BENEDETTO CROCE:
COLLECTED WORKS

Volume 2

CROCE, THE KING AND THE ALLIES

CROCE, THE KING AND THE ALLIES

Extracts from a diary by Benedetto Croce, July 1943 - June 1944

BENEDETTO CROCE

LONDON AND NEW YORK

First published in English in 1950 by George Allen & Unwin Ltd.

This edition first published in 2019
by Routledge
2 Park Square, Milton Park, Abingdon, Oxon OX14 4RN

and by Routledge
52 Vanderbilt Avenue, New York, NY 10017

Routledge is an imprint of the Taylor & Francis Group, an informa business

British Library Cataloguing in Publication Data
A catalogue record for this book is available from the British Library

ISBN: 978-0-367-10994-3 (Set)
ISBN: 978-0-429-05271-2 (Set) (ebk)
ISBN: 978-0-367-14001-4 (Volume 2) (hbk)
ISBN: 978-0-367-14011-3 (Volume 2) (pbk)
ISBN: 978-0-429-02964-6 (Volume 2) (ebk)

Publisher's Note
The publisher has gone to great lengths to ensure the quality of this reprint but points out that some imperfections in the original copies may be apparent.

Disclaimer
The publisher has made every effort to trace copyright holders and would welcome correspondence from those they have been unable to trace.

CROCE, THE KING AND THE ALLIES

EXTRACTS FROM A DIARY BY BENEDETTO CROCE

JULY 1943—JUNE 1944

Translated by

SYLVIA SPRIGGE

GEORGE ALLEN & UNWIN LTD

RUSKIN HOUSE MUSEUM STREET LONDON

FIRST PUBLISHED IN 1950

PRINTED IN GREAT BRITAIN
in 11pt. Baskerville type
BY BRADFORD AND DICKENS
LONDON, W.C. 1

DEDICATION

To my city of Naples
which has neither sought nor desired
autonomy or separation
religiously faithful
to that idea of national unity
which its men of 1799
were among the first to espouse
I dedicate this diary of a period
in which although in fact separated
we continually thought of Italy
and longed to be united again

NOTE

THE following diary extracts were published in the *Quaderni della Critica* in 1946 and 1947, with the following Foreword:

"Historical accounts are beginning to appear in print of the nine months from early September 1943 to June 1944, a period when Government and political party activity could only take place in southern Italy and in the islands. I thought I might correct and integrate certain errors and certain omissions not easy to avoid in such accounts, with these notes from a diary, which I have been keeping these last forty years in a fairly brief form, at the beginning or end of my day, and whose purpose has been to note the course of my literary work. But after July 25th 1943, owing to the rush of events, the diary gradually filled with notes on political matters. In the following pages are extracts without the literary and private notes, of which I have left only a few in the early pages so that the character and nature of the Diary may be kept in mind. The political notes were a part of it, and at first were entered occasionally and almost involuntarily. Some details of little importance I have left in, being desirous and careful not to offend the susceptibilities or rouse the resentment of any one, for my purpose is solely that which I have already outlined. I do not know whether I have always succeeded in this, despite the goodwill which I have put into it."

In making the present volume I have added an appendix of some of the many documents I possess which refer to the attempt in Naples (noted in September and October 1943) to form a Corps of Italian volunteers. I take this occasion to express my ever-grateful thanks to the American General Donovan who, when I first barely mentioned the idea, greeted it without comment, studied it in his mind and then proposed it and fathered it with the American and British authorities. Really generous and high-minded actions are not forgotten even if they meet with failure.

B.C.

Naples,

November 1947

THE DIARY

Sorrento, July 25th, 1943

In the morning, historical reading; but in the afternoon, visits from friends, Parente, both the Morellis, Zanotti Bianco, Petaccia. The Dohrns are here too. I was tired and had gone to bed at eleven o'clock when a telephone call from Signorina Elena di Serracapriola's villa brought the news that Mussolini had resigned and that the new Government had been entrusted to Badoglio by the King. Parente and the Morellis, who had gone away half an hour ago, on hearing the news also arrived, jubilant, and we talked of the event. Back to bed, but I could not close my eyes till four o'clock or later. The feeling I have is of liberation from an evil which weighed upon the heart's core; derivative evils and dangers remain, but that evil will not return.

July 26th

To-day, repercussions from yesterday's event. Many visits, people asking for news, conjectures, an occasional piece of reliable news. Went to the Lieutenant who commands the Carabineers here to get R.P. released. He had been arrested with others for having taken part in the attack on the Fascist headquarters in Sorrento. Was given a hopeful reply. During the rest of the day I was unable to do anything, being interrupted in whatever reading I embarked upon.

July 27th

Slept little to-night also, from midnight to 4 a.m. My thoughts are concentrated on the fate of Italy. Fascism seems already a thing of the past to me, a cycle that is closed, and I have no taste for the pleasures of vendetta. But Italy is still a painful problem. Have received 120 pages of a reprint of my *History of the Kingdom of Naples*; have begun to re-read the *Niebelungen* and made a few additions to what I have written. Otherwise to-day, also, anxious waiting for news and much distress and feeling of rebellion at words spoken against Italy by English statesmen, who are perhaps preparing to saddle us with the burden of our disastrous war, in the name of justice and morality. And yet, once at the cross-roads, there never was but one course for Italians, to choose defeat rather than apparent victory by the side of the kind of allies whom Mussolini had inflicted on Italy, when he sold Italy and its future and co-operated in enslaving every one in Europe.

July 28th

Rosati, Morelli and Parente over from Naples to ask me for some suggestions and for a manuscript, even if already written and printed for restricted circulation, or unprinted, but suitable for these days. Other visitors also. In between, was able to revise some of the proofs for the next number of *Critica*. I find the spectacle of rapid political changeovers going on just now are not unexpected, but always repugnant, and yet they also seem to have something sincere and healthy, some expansion, a pleasure in the return of the word and the appearances of liberty, and one feels that Fascist oppression and corruption did not altogether succeed in driving the memory of liberty from the hearts of Italians.

August 2nd

Wrote some brief notes of an appeal, to be published in a small pamphlet, for the reconstitution of an Italian Liberal Party.[1] Wrote several letters for friends who are going to Rome, Turin and Florence. Corrected proofs of *Storia di Napoli*. Revised part of the typed copy of other writings of Blanch, rewritten by me. Bombing of Naples has started again, heavy yesterday and extremely heavy now, as I write (about eleven p.m.). From here we watch anxiously.

August 3rd

Woke up, as often happens these days, after little more than four hours' sleep, stayed in bed thinking, not pleasantly. This reduces my alacrity for the rest of the day. Nevertheless, I finished revising the extended Blanch and read variously. Vinciguerra, freed from imprisonment, came to see me and we talked of current events.

August 4th

Wrote an open letter to Bergamini for the *Giornale d'Italia* under

[1] This and similar work is collected in the volume *Per una nuova vita dell' Italia* (Naples, Ricciardi, 1944), pp. 87–108.

the heading of "Liberty over and above all." Wrote letters and revised proofs. Awful bombing of Naples in the afternoon, right over the centre of the city. Such a fall of bombs that the house we live in here, across the bay, shook.

August 5th

Got through long and extensive correspondence, also wrote letters on behalf of two German men of letters who came to ask for some protection from persecution of their fellow-countrymen, which they believe is about to break out. Naturally I did what I could, gave them statements and offered to guarantee them. I was back again on elaborating Blanch when friends arrived from Naples and told us of the horrible destruction after yesterday's big bombs, which dropped all over the city. The house opposite ours in Naples is in ruins, and the greater part of the Church of Santa Chiara is burnt out, that museum of the Angevins, and all or nearly all the memorials in it are destroyed. Our house is standing, but the roof and the balconies have been badly damaged, and a fire began but was got under. In the evening went on revising proofs of *Storia.*

August 13th

Prepared letter for Morelli, who is leaving this week for Rome. Am much annoyed at the behaviour of those who belong to the Party of so-called Action, who make a hotchpotch of contradictory ideas, produce impracticable programmes and deliver stupid and factious accusations and excommunications. Since they mix my name up with their pronouncements I have decided to write to Casati in Rome so that he be informed that the Liberal Party has been reconstituted, pure and simple, in the tradition of Cavour, as it was when Ruffini and I and others led it and when it was suppressed by Fascism in 1925. Elaborated other writings of Blanch. Read a little, but distractedly. The destruction of Italian cities and their monuments leaves me comfortless.

August 14th

Omodeo has returned from Rome bringing rather pessimistic news. Went to pay a visit to G.B., who has arrived from Rome, and from her learned more detailed news about Badoglio's negotiations to get Italy out of the present absurd situation.

August 15th

Revised and sent off proofs of the book on *Poesia di Dante.* Having read proposals which have flowered in the minds of many that I should be nominated as President of the Italian Academy, I have sent an article to the *Giornale d'Italia* on the need for abolishing this Academy and for re-establishing the *Accademia dei Lincei.* Got through business connected with our house in Naples, and with a ground-floor room I was asked for by someone now without a dwelling, and got it opened at once. In the evening worked again on the elaboration of Blanch.

August 18th

Revised and sent off two pamphlets: *Propositi e Speranze* and *Libertà e Giustizia.*

August 20th

Am listless and sleepy, as I have never been before. I sleep little at nights: before me I always see the ruin of Italy, and the news of Giovanni Laterza's bad health, rapidly deteriorating, depresses me. When they brought the news of the fall of Fascism to his sick-bed on July 26th, he ordered the words "God be praised" to be written at the head of all letters and bills of that day. In the afternoon, as best I could, took up the threads of work in hand, including the revised elaboration of Blanch. The *Giornale d'Italia* has printed my article on the Italian Academy despite the veto of the censors which Bergamini has overridden. But other articles on the subject are forbidden. I am told that the King said, "The Academy is not to be tampered with any more than the Senate." But the Senate too, unworthy and corrupt as it is, will have to be 'tampered with.'

August 24th

In a newspaper I happened to see the news of Laterza's death. A little later a four-day old telegram from the family arrived. Alas, this unhappy news is not unexpected, but we hoped and imagined that for some time he would still be among us. I suffer and feel indignant about the attitude of the English, their exhortations, requests and threats that we should do what would already have been done had it been possible to do it. In the afternoon worked again on Blanch, but had to stop in the evening owing to the effects

[2] See *Pagine Politiche* (Bari, 1945), pp. 41–8.

of the almost daily bombing of Naples. To-day's raid has seen the power station damaged, so that electric light is off all along the coast.

August 27th

Received a letter from G.B., who tells me that agreement with the Anglo-Americans has been reached, of which we shall soon see the results. The news has so excited me that I have been unable to do anything during the rest of the day. Joy? No, but the sense that one is getting out of the jungle into a painful but straight road.

August 28th

To-day too has gone in very little work and much speculation and resting with feet up, between yesterday's news and the doubt that it was mere speculation.

August 29th

Very gloomy day because I heard that the main pipe of Naples had been hit and the city is without water. In the evening no electricity here.

September 3rd

News of the Anglo-American landing in Calabria.

September 4th

A friend tells me of a telephone message from Rome: "The patient has recovered. Tell Senator Croce"—which we interpreted as news of the conclusion of the expected agreement.

September 7th

As usual, fearful rumours about the fate of Naples and of Italy. Meanwhile I cannot believe the news from Rome to be speculation. It comes from a serious man, who would not have taken the trouble to telephone me a mere rumour.

September 8th

As I was returning home from a brief walk at 6.30 p.m. Adelina told me that she heard on the wireless that the armistice with the Anglo-Americans has been made.

September 9th

Omodeo came over from Naples, full of his new office as Rector of the University of Naples and of the inauguration at which he made a fine and useful call to colleagues and students.

September 10th

In the afternoon entertained new hopes and fears on account of military events and of episodes showing the Italian reaction against the Germans. In the evening heard of the German occupation of Rome and the flight of the King and Badoglio, who have withdrawn to safety. Anxiety on behalf of so many of our friends there, all involved in opposing Fascism.

September 11th

We watched Germans fire their guns from the coast at Torre Annunziata upon a motor boat carrying passengers and goods and later heard that ten people were thus killed. Friends coming from Naples bring news that Naples has been occupied by the Germans and that there has been fighting among the people, with dead and wounded.

September 12th

Some American soldiers have arrived in Sorrento. Raimondo, who went out exploring yesterday, came back to-day with rumours about the situation and about immediate developments. No news from Naples, though Dohrn, who came last night, maintains that there has not been a proper occupation, but that certain German units have returned, and that fights occurred owing to nervousness and misunderstandings. Anyway, nothing is certain. In the evening news that Mussolini has been freed by the Germans.

September 13th

Raimondo off on his explorations again. We are completely isolated. No post for a week, no papers from Naples for two days and probably they are not coming out; no communication by sea or road with Naples these last two days. From to-day we are without light and without water, owing to English bombing of Torre dell'Annunziata, and the failure of electric power. So there has been no wireless since noon and we know nothing at all, and all we hear is the noise of guns and explosions. We have not even been able to hear the speech which, according to one rumour, Prometheus unbound was to make to the Italian people at 6 p.m. Signor Gugliucci, a friend from the Cilento mountains, who has been here these last weeks, having heard that former local Fascists are getting lively again, and worried about some anonymous letters threatening me during the past few days, has set a guard about the house where we live, and to-night he wants to sleep here and has even got hold of some hand grenades! Corrected most of an essay by Blanch on the history of legislation, which I rewrote from beginning to end and Lydia typed. Went to bed early, there being no light and, thank heavens, I felt better for the rest, despite the gunfire on the coast.

September 14th

Finished correcting Blanch's essay and did other minor work. Plans for the formation here in Sorrento of a Committee to meet the dangers of this uncertain situation, seeing that Sorrento is still without either Germans or Anglo-Americans, and there is fear of sudden action by the former or by remaining Fascists emboldened by recent events (freeing of Mussolini, occupation by the Germans). Above all we are distressed about the local population, which has had no bread now for several days. In the evening Raimondo, who is now with Anglo-American headquarters, sent me injunctions to betake myself immediately to Capri with my family, and I have answered that I could not go, both for practical and for moral reasons, not wishing to spread panic among the population here by making a kind of flight.

Capri, September 15th

I had settled down to read the manuscript of a work by Alda on Gongora when I was first interrupted by various questions and people asking for advice about the Committee whose formation was announced yesterday, which should start working to-day. I had started reading again when two girls walked into my study. They were the daughters of the Fascist ex-mayor of Sorrento. They were crying, shouting and making much ado because their father had gone to Maiori to the Anglo-Americans on behalf of this town, mainly to ask urgently for food and had then been detained there. I had just calmed them down, promising I would set about getting him free, and had advised them to behave in a more practical way, when we received a telephone call that a floating mine had been found under our villa and that we must go away at once so that it might be caught and exploded. We scattered in the garden and wasted more time until we were told the danger was past. Inside the house, I had just begun reading again at about six o'clock when a series of people arrived, some to talk about the Committee, others, Fascists, to assure me of their virtues and worthiness. When they had gone and I had begun reading again Alda came (about 7.30 p.m.) to tell me that Brindisi, my friend and police commissioner in Capri, together with a British officer, were in the garden and wished to speak to me. I went to meet them and took them into my study. The Englishman (who was a naval officer called Gallegos, of Spanish origin) told me that German patrols were nearby in the hills and that an action was expected in the course of which I was to be captured and taken, as others have been taken in Salerno and elsewhere, as a hostage. And this he said, apart from all the rest (I thought of all the lies and betrayals they would have attributed to me), would be an instrument of blackmail in their hands. Brindisi added his own exhortations and persuasiveness, and so I decided to go with them to Capri, taking with me papers and a few other things I was able to collect in a hurry, because speed was essential. There never being any light here, it was all done by the glow of an odd candle and matches. (Later, Adelina told me that while we were in the garden a peasant down from the hills had given her a note from a friend in Naples which urged me to leave Sorrento quickly, but that she had not shown it to me, knowing of my contrary resolution.) About 9 p.m. we embarked, myself with Elena, Lydia and Sylvia, in an Italian motor launch lent to Capri by Commander Michelagnoli, and with us Brindisi and the English officer. Adelina and Alda stayed behind to gather together other indispensable things and to hand over the house to Gigliucci and to Omodeo, who is then going to join his family at Positano. They will be brought to Capri to-morrow. We arrived here about 10.30 p.m., and went up to the Morgano Hotel in a car sent down by the Admiral, and after dinner and talk with Brindisi and Fausto Nicolini, who is in Capri with his family, we went to bed soon after eleven o'clock.

September 16th

Got up at six and wrote letters to Adelina, Alda and the others who stayed with them in Sorrento. Then with Nicolini came Tarchiani and Cianca, back from America, whom I had not seen for ten years, and with them I talked for three good hours, giving and receiving news of Italian matters and finding myself in agreement with them about people I had known, and they had known too, in France and in America. At 3 p.m. Brindisi set out for Sorrento again in a motor launch belonging to Admiral Barone, who has come here with his son. Half-way across they met friends who told them that the Germans had arrived at Sorrento and so persuaded them to turn back. Barone's son alone went on in the dinghy to see how things were and to get news of his mother and sister left behind in Sorrento. Later on, perhaps by way of embroidering these events, the news went round that the Germans made straight for the Villa del Tritone, thinking to find me there, and had surrounded it. I had an hour of atrocious anxiety thinking of the ill-treatment or imprisonment of my wife and my daughter. But fortunately Barone's son came back from his survey and told us that nothing new has happened in Sorrento, that the Germans have not arrived yet, although they are rebuilding the arch of the bridge over the Selano, which the Americans had blown up. I was anxiously awaiting the morning when Brindisi was to renew to-day's expedition, interrupted by the aforesaid incident, but my good friend, unbeknown to me, had set off again in the night, accompanied by Major Munthe (son of Axel Munthe) and by Tarchiani, in a motor launch lent him by an Italian officer. He had put in at Sorrento, and although someone shouted to him not to go on, because the Germans were there, he went round to the villa, had it quickly opened, and brought Adelina and Alda here. They suddenly arrived at 2 a.m.

September 17th

In the morning a visit from an American journalist, Kearney, who asked me some political questions, which I answered as best I could, what with being tired, not having slept and it being stiflingly hot. While Elena was helping to translate my answers into English, the English Admiral, J. B. Morse, came to visit me with his aide, Richard Long, and we had a short conversation. The lieutenant asked me who were the dangerous or Fascist people in Sorrento, and I asked to be excused because I could not, in my old age, begin doing things I had never done in the course of my life, to which the lieutenant agreed and said he well understood. The Germans left over there were mentioned in the conversation; but the Dohrn family, although attached to their country, has been noted as 'neutral.' In the evening a much famed journalist, Knickerbocker, came to say a lot of kind things to me, and then talked for a long time with my daughters, and wanting to give proof of his admiration, he wrote some lines by which to remember him in a copy of Shakespeare which they had with them.

September 18th

Various rumours about what is happening in Sorrento. Doria's brother, who has come here, tells us that the Germans only drove through Sorrento in lorries to find supplies, and are said to have taken all the food from the Minerva Hotel on the Point. In the evening that disgraceful Mussolini spoke on the wireless; my daughters were strong enough to listen to the whole of his speech and then reported it to me in broad outline. To-morrow we shall leave the Morgano Hotel and move to the Albertini's villa, relations of Elena's and friends of ours who have stayed on in Rome.

September 19th

In the morning, at Brindisi's invitation, went with Adelina and two of my daughters to a requiem mass in the cathedral for Allied and Italian soldiers killed in the war. Have found a well-furnished library in the Albertini's villa. Sadness on account of Lucetti's death. He once made an attempt on Mussolini's life and, freed a few days ago from confinement on the island of Ventotene, he has been killed by machine-gun fire on the way over from Capri, whether on the journey or during a stop at Ischia I do not know. Those who met him here when he came through, like Tarchiani and Cianca, admired and greatly appreciated his moderation, his modesty and his judgment.

September 20th

News of Raimondo from American officers, with whose command he now is. The Nazi and Fascist wireless, having announced four days ago that "B. Croce and others like him who have abused the patience of the regime will be severely punished," the English wireless has to-day announced that I was taken to safety by English officers.

September 21st

In the evening Zaniboni (sentenced for attempted assassination of Mussolini), his daughter and a friend and fellow-prisoner of his on Ventotene, Duke Camerini of Ferrara, came. Also two young Neapolitans from the American camp, who are going to Ischia, and from there propose to make an expedition to Naples. In the evening Raimondo, and soon after Max Salvadori, brother of Joyce Salvadori, and now a British officer serving under the name of Captain Sylvester.

September 22nd

Raimondo has left again. Suffocating heat continues. Tight feeling about the heart for Naples in the hands of the Germans. From here we hear explosions and see fires, and get rumours of people killed, devastation and looting. General Donovan and a journalist called Whitaker, together with an American officer called Tomkins, whom I got to know in the last few days and who has been in Italy previously for a long time, came to see me. The General told me that large supplies have been prepared for Naples, to be landed ten or fifteen days after the occupation. He said it might be a good thing if I let this be known in Naples. I said I would spread the news among people I shall see, but that I have no means of communicating with Naples. Similarly, with another of his suggestions that the Neapolitans should try to prevent the Germans from destroying the port. Whitaker offered me presses, paper and ink with which to print a paper here! General Donovan asked me how the spirit of the Italians was, and I said that what all the best Italians wanted, and what would most encourage them, would be permission to form a combatant legion under the Italian flag to co-operate with the Anglo-American armies in liberating Italian soil from the Germans; and then, when he asked me whether there was anybody who could command such a legion, I gave him General Pavone's name, a man of an old southern family, a patriot and a liberal, and presently a member of the Party of Action.

September 23rd

Captain Manley came back early to-day from Ischia and brought me news of what has been happening and is now going on in Naples. The American officer Tomkins, who accompanied my two visitors of yesterday, came back to tell me that General Donovan is very much in with Roosevelt and is his representative with the Army, and that John Whitaker, of the *Chicago Daily News,* is a most reliable journalist, and as correspondent in Rome had furnished the American public with all they knew about Fascism; he had been in touch with Ciano and in 1941 had been sent to an internment camp, later being exchanged for Italian journalists and allowed to leave. Also learnt in the course of conversation that the Anglo-Americans for the present are only putting out a pretty vague programme, setting up regimes in Italy and in Europe which stand half-way between Conservatism and Communism. What sort of regimes will they be? They do not sound plain liberal regimes, because if they were they would not need such vague and circumlocutionary definition. I also learnt that the word 'Fascism' is interpreted in the most various and different ways by the American public, and that in some of these ways it rallies the most staunch defenders round it. Its intrinsic logic and its brutal reality are not generally made clear. Both in England and in America Liberals are very apprehensive lest a Fascist temperament should develop and be encouraged by the war, and no one knows what will become of so many people who have held commands and will want to go on commanding after the war, and will not easily return to the order which existed before the war. In the evening the German-Fascist wireless announced the miserable Ministry which Mussolini has nominated, in which Graziani alone stands out.

September 24th

Raimondo, General Pavone, Tarchiani, Cianca and then other visitors came, among whom Zaniboni, his daughter and Camerini. I went aside with the first three and we read a page of notes from someone at the American command, from which it appears that what I said to General Donovan about the part Italy wants to play in the war against Germany has had an unexpected effect, for General Donovan has supported my proposal with the American Command. We decided meanwhile to constitute ourselves into a provisional Committee with the name "National Front of Liberation," and to reply by letter to the invitation implied in the page of notes which I have by me. The letter has been written in English, typewritten, and signed by myself and Pavone. I have undertaken to write a manifesto for broadcast to the Italian people; General Pavone is to make an appeal for volunteers for his legions.

September 25th

Have prepared the above manifesto, but have not had the energy to draft it because of what I hear and see in Naples, which weighs on my spirit.

September 26th

In the afternoon, some three hours or more conversation with Matthews, who was a correspondent in Rome from 1939–41 and is now a war correspondent.

September 27th

In the evening a high American officer came to make my personal acquaintance, the son of that very dear and regretted author, Spingarn, of *Literary Criticism in the Renaissance.*

September 28th

Have seen a Neapolitan anti-Fascist, bold, resolute and very useful. But he is extremely ingenuous and seems to reduce everything to his membership of a party which calls itself 'Of Action' or 'Free Italy.' As Spingarn asked me to enlighten him about the various Italian parties, I said that this Party of Action was composed of 'Liberal Democrats' or 'Radicals'; but the other man, who was present, and had come from Salerno with Spingarn, leaped up and shouted that it was the strongest and most powerful party in Italy, that it had 'the masses' with it, etc. I finally got him to understand that, whether or not this was true, Spingarn was asking me what was the idea or what the programme of the party was, and that therefore I had defined it as best I could by giving it a place among the 'Liberal Democrats.' But he protested that it was not 'Liberal-Democrat' but 'Social-Democrat'; to which I, with honest surprise, explained to him that 'Social-Democracy' or *Sozialdemokratie* was synonomous to 'Socialism' and that an Italian Socialist Party already existed. His answer was as follows: "Yes, but it has not got the masses, we have them!" Naturally I interrupted our dialogue, because Spingarn does not understand Italian, and I went on giving him the information he wanted, in the way which seemed rational to me.

September 29th

In the evening Raimondo came with Lt. Munthe and we took

decisions on political matters. We got Munthe to read the manifesto and he was both convinced and moved by it.

September 30th

During the day, political affairs; had to write letters and make notes about them. The news is about that Naples has been occupied by the Americans. Several young men who have been travelling between Naples and the islands went off to Naples. Agreed with Raimondo and Tarchiani that they will both leave to-morrow morning for Salerno, and go from there to Torchiara to inform Pavone, and then on to Taranto or to Brindisi to talk with Marshall Badoglio, to whom I have given them letters of introduction, since he was a colleague of mine in the Senate and I have met him there occasionally in Casati's company without having closer relations with him. The wireless to-night quoted several sentences from my conversation of the other day with Matthews, especially my reference to Goethe's saying, which I had applied to Fascism: "Nothing is more terrifying than active ignorance."

October 1st

The wireless gives news of agreements between Badoglio and the Anglo-American authorities about the war against the Germans in Italy. This might include our plan of action inside a vaster plan; in any case, we have done our duty and not waited for others to get going. Raimondo and Tarchiani have left together to talk to Badoglio and I hope that they will carry out the programme we planned. I spent time roughly arranging and reordering into various parcels all the many letters I have received from all over Italy in the month of August. Since the early days of September, by reason of railroad interruptions, due to political events, all post has ceased, nor does any one know, except for southern Italy, when it will be re-established. Desultory reading during the day, but always in deep anxiety for what has happened in Naples, of which no direct news. Only one person, Schmidt, an Austrian painter, back in Capri, having escaped from the Germans who for several months used him as their interpreter, has brought me a letter from Dohrn with horrible news in it, especially about thousands of young men whom the Germans and the Fascists are said to have impressed in the streets and taken away to work for them on military installations in occupied Italy. In the evening Zaniboni and Camerini came to see me and the latter told me about his position. During August, though free, he had not moved from Ponza, not wanting to recognize Badoglio's government. Once in Capri he had presented some American officer (and having done this, thought the matter was finished) with a proposal for forming a Legion against the Germans, commanded by himself, directly under American command, but with equality, that is, as an ally: a republican legion. I explained to him at length why his whole design had ended in nothing; something different is needed (this I didn't tell him) to bridge the gulf between a beaten enemy and an ally; why one could not expect nor ask the English and the Americans to welcome our Republican programme and thereby encourage internal division; why any proposal for an armed corps would have to be communicated to Badoglio and discussed with him, etc., etc.; and why now, after the agreement with Badoglio for action against the Germans, the voluntary legions could not but follow the example given by Garibaldi in 1859 and in 1866, that is, be manned by Italians of every party with a common ideal, fighting alongside the regular Army, to get the foreigner out. Zaniboni was not persuaded by this clear reasoning, for he went on repeating that he felt himself left outside, that he had been taken in (one does not know by whom or how), etc.

October 2nd

In the evening Camerini came back and talked again of Zaniboni's and his own idea that a legion should be formed, politically independent of Badoglio's government; I exerted myself to persuade him that the thing was impossible in practice.

October 3rd

This morning the wireless announces a proclamation by the King about the war against the Germans; but the King's intervention leaves me cold, and I fear that it will give no value or strength to the movement; the impulse must come from elsewhere. Why on earth has not this unfortunate man at least abdicated and left the throne to his son, who is not so directly responsible or so gravely compromised as he is?

October 4th

Woke up shortly after 3 a.m. and could not go to sleep again. Thought over the war, international law, other similar concepts and wondered, under the terrible passion of these days, which parts are to be morally condemned; but my conclusions confirmed even more firmly the old theory that war is not to be judged either morally or juridically, and that when there is war there is no other possibility and no other duty but to seek to win it. About 9 p.m. Cassandro came from Naples. He briefly gave me news of what has happened in Naples during a week of the German occupation. He will come back to-morrow to give me further details.

October 5th

Several young men, refugees from Rome and from northern Italy, came. In the afternoon I unexpectedly found Signora Joyce Salvadori, now Signora Lussu, in my study, who had courageously crossed the German lines and come from Rome.

October 6th

Spoke at length with young Cassandro about Neapolitan things. In the evening another long talk with the Salvadori, because she, in the name of her husband and his friends, asks that our war activity against the Germans should not only not take any account of the King's government and of Badoglio, but oppose them. I tried to show her that this was impossible; that the Anglo-Americans had made the armistice with Badoglio's government and had relations with it and had recognized it as the legal Government of Italy; we must form battalions of volunteers who will swear loyalty neither to the King nor to Badoglio, nor make demonstrations for or against the monarchy, but solely think of getting the Germans out and so vindicate their honour.

October 7th

In the afternoon Raimondo came back and brought me the typed copy of the conversations which he and Tarchiani have had in Brindisi with Marshall Badoglio, whom they immediately saw, after showing my credentials. With Badoglio they quickly came to full agreement that we should act not independently of the King's government, and that he, Badoglio, would not put any obstacles in our way. In the evening a big gathering in our house of the refugees who are here.

October 8th

Signora Salvadori, who has been with us all the time during these days, left again to-day with Raimondo and others for Naples, whence she will return to Rome, passing through the German lines again. With Tarchiani, with whom I agree in ideas and in political judgment, we prepared the necessary papers.

October 9th

Raimondo came back with General Pavone and an air officer, Moscatelli, who has escaped from the Germans and the Fascists and come here to enlist. The Anglo-American command has accepted our proposals and requests concerning the formation of fighting units under the Italian flag and commanded by Pavone. We took some decisions about carrying out these plans. Have kept all the documents concerning these arrangements.

October 10th

Have had to revise the proclamation which is to be published on the formation of fighting units, in order to bring it into harmony with events of the last few days and with the agreement with Badoglio. From news I have received and documents I have seen, I have become convinced that the King and the vassalage which surrounds him seek the salvation of the monarchy by means of the support which they hope to find among the majority of ex-Fascists, whom they protect as best they can from interference and from being deprived of their salaries and jobs. All that is asked is a profession of monarchist faith; every one, even Communists, are then accepted. This game which is supposed to gloss over the deplorable conduct of the King under Fascism, will not, I think, be successful, and in any case we shall be vigilant and defeat it. I have always regarded the monarchy as being useful to Italy; but it is not our fault if the Savoy monarchy has lost all prestige, as every one says and hears said. Tarchiani came and I read to him my revised edition of the proclamation; it pleased him and he made a copy of it to take to Naples. He stayed a few hours with us and we talked of the past and the present.

October 11th

Tarchiani has written a *communiqué*, a compendium of what we have done since the idea of the fighting units was accepted and begun. I begged him to withhold my name and to give me no outstanding place in the national committee of the 'Liberation Front' which we have made; and this he did. In the evening Matthews came back and we talked at length; he asked me for an article on Fascism or on Marxism for the *New York Times*.

October 12th

Tarchiani left for Naples to see to the publication of the proclamation and propaganda for the fighting units. Cianca stayed here, still suffering from a fever which will not stop. He worries that he cannot work with us now that there is so much to do in matters in which certainly he, as a valiant orator, would do extremely well. With Matthews came three American journalists, who took innumerable photographs of me and my family for the review *Life*.

October 13th

Tried to begin the article for the *New York Times*, but could not get on with it. I find is so repellent and wearisome still to be talking of Fascism. And yet, I must write it. In the afternoon Matthews gave me notes of one of our conversations (which I had not thought of as an interview). Everything that I think on the question of the monarchy and the person of the King is toned down. Among other things an anecdote is inserted which I told in conversation, in order to clearly explain my thought, which is: not to pass judgment on the person of the King, because I cannot now, nor perhaps can any one, pass judgment *ex informata conscientia*; and a king has the right to be treated as we would treat any private person. I simply note, as a fact which must be taken into account, and seriously into account, that he has lost prestige. To this end and to underline my view, which was not intended to be a moral judgment, I told a fairly drastic anecdote about General Ellena, at the battle of Adua in 1896, and how he was withdrawn, having lost prestige through no fault of his own.

I made a few slight revisions to his notes, but then decided to send them back to him with a letter in which I rely on his tact and beg him to consider whether it is expedient at the present moment to raise questions of monarchy or anti-monarchy in Italy and outside Italy. In the afternoon Minister Piccardi, back from Brindisi, came to see me, and with him were Arangio Ruiz and Morra di Lavriano. Piccardi asked me whether, in view of the imminent liberation of

Rome, it would not be expedient to form a political Ministry in place of the present one, which is not at all military; whether Badoglio should be kept as President or Head of the Government, or substituted; what attitude to take over the question of the monarchy. I answered (1) that it seemed necessary to form a political Ministry; (2) that I thought that, since the only urgent problem now was the war against the Germans, it was certainly not desirable to remove Badoglio from his post and that both on account of his military capacity and because of his decisive attitude in this crisis, against Fascism and against the Germans, he was, more than any other man, the most suitable; (3) that the institutional question must be put aside, for it would be solved in the course of events, and we must try to get Badoglio to advise the King, when he gets back to Rome, to abdicate in favour of his son. Piccardi declared that he was in agreement with me on all these points. He is going back to Naples, where he will talk to the others in the Liberation Front, that is with Raimondo and Tarchiani, who will inform him of our plan and especially of our arrangement with Badoglio, to which I only made a vague reference.

October 14th

Have written the article on "Fascism as a World Danger" for the *New York Times*.[3] But fell into a sad depression because of the frightful news that the Germans, after soaking the castle of San Paolo Belsito in petrol, have burned it down. Thither all the archives of the State of Naples had been taken as a precaution against raids, all the most ancient and precious archives, the parchments, the Angevin registers, the Aragon chancellory papers, the Farnese papers, the records of the trials of the Summary Court, the census, etc., etc.—all the papers on which I too had worked in the past and from which some of my books are made, all the documents of the history of the Kingdom of Naples. My feelings are like those of someone who has lost his dearest friend, and my mind measures the immensity of the loss for our traditions and for historical knowledge. Nor is there any remedy, nor any reprisal which could satisfy; and meanwhile we are barely at the beginning of the systematic destruction which these people of barbarous instincts and pedantic mind are proposing to wreak on Italy, not only the Italy that is industrial and on its economic life, but on Italy's ideal value as a

[3] *Op. cit.*, pp. 21–5.

mistress of history and of the arts. Yesterday Parente and Cassandro came from Naples and I talked with them at length, receiving and giving information about the events of the last few weeks and establishing the procedure about the matters in hand.

October 15th

Col. T. arrived, whom I had known many years ago in Turin, an anti-Fascist, and a friend of my friends. He has fled from Rome to Naples in order to take part in the war, and since he said that service in the Royal Army was distasteful to him, I told him to get in touch with Pavone's volunteer units. Two American officers arrived from reconnoitring units, who were parachuted on Rome very recently in order to get in touch with the anti-Fascists there, and hearing that I was in Capri came to find me. One of them, Lloyd Fangel, is a close friend and almost a spiritual son of Livingstone, from whom he brought me greetings, and who had scolded him some years ago because, passing through Naples, he had not stopped to call on me. The other is a Major Roy Tozier; both are students of philosophy and know my books. The affectionate ways of these two young men—they practically caressed me—was moving.

October 16th

My sadness continued and a sense of inadequacy at how much must be borne while suffering and working. Nevertheless, I recollected myself in meditation and was able to get through some small literary tasks. Floriano Del Secolo came from Naples. I spent the evening with him and discussed how to sow the seeds of a paper in Naples which would be independent of business interests. The suspension of existing newspapers for lack of paper, and because of the Anglo-American occupation, offers an opportunity. Was much distressed to learn of the opposition to our attempt to form volunteer units or fighting corps, not only by Badoglio but by monarchical elements.

October 17th

Wrote a letter to Whitaker, head of the propaganda office (or 'psychological warfare'), with the Military Command of the First Army, proposing that the new paper or sheet should have a new title and should be entrusted to Del Secolo as its sole editor.

Sorrento, October 19th

This morning, accompanied by Brindisi and Nicolini, on a motor launch of the Royal Navy, we returned in less than half an hour to Sorrento, where we arrived at 9.30 a.m. We found the house in perfect order owing to the care of a friend. But in the evening, from 5.30 p.m. onwards, we were in the dark, and by the light of wicks and lanterns we succeeded in dining, but hardly in reading or writing.

October 21st

Raimondo, General Pavone and Caracciolo di Castagneto came to tell me that they are leaving to-morrow morning for Bari to meet Sforza, who has been brought directly to Brindisi. Tarchiani has gone on ahead of them and will have told him about the situation. Gave a letter to Raimondo in which I tell Sforza of my anxiety for the dangerous political attitude which the King has taken up, or which those who counsel and guide him make him take up.

October 22nd

From an American journalist who came to ask me whether Sforza was with me, I had news of the German air raid on Naples which we watched from here yesterday, and which was stoutly met by the Anglo-American defences, so that there was only slight damage to some houses and, unfortunately, a few casualties.

October 23rd

At 7 p.m. another German air raid on Naples, a long one, uninterruptedly met by anti-aircraft fire.

October 24th

In the afternoon Omodeo came to see me and asked me to go to Naples to be present at the granting of an *honoris causa* degree to the American General Clark, in order to demonstrate my solidarity with Omodeo as Rector (which meets with some opposition) and to say some words on behalf of the University. I agreed, but asked him to put off departure till the morning. So he stayed the night at Sorrento.

October 25th

Left at 6 a.m. We arrived in Naples about 8 a.m. Taking advantage of a few free hours I walked through some of the city's streets, and visited a couple of second-hand booksellers and then took part in a meeting of members of the Liberal Party. The University ceremony was carried out in a most serious and dignified manner. General Clark spoke very noble words. Omodeo had put me at the presidential table, and naturally I received great applause in a place where for many years I had not been able to show myself. In the afternoon went back with Elena to Sorrento where I found Sforza's son waiting for me, whom I had not seen for ten years, and a friend of his, the engineer Almagia.

October 27th

Eight or nine members of the Naples Committee of Liberation, formed of several parties, came to see me. I spoke freely with them for about three hours, but in all truth pointing out that they have committed a series of errors beginning with their having included in the Committee, besides the representatives of the six parties, representatives of the ex-combatants and the disabled, which is like a grammatical error in policy, because the individual ex-combatants and disabled are already inscribed in the six parties. Moreover they had committed the error of protesting against the formation of volunteer units, raising the question of the monarchy and the republic, which can be of no possible use but to damp the ardour of the volunteers. I said that we should accept men whether monarchists or republicans, following the example of Garibaldi. Thirdly, they had voted against my proposal of a newspaper to be run by Del Secolo, without having even remotely understood what it was all about, and having approached it as a matter of courtesy or compassion. In all these things they did not contradict me, but recognized that these errors had been made; and after we had exchanged our thoughts on Neapolitan problems they went away satisfied, and left me friendly and affectionately disposed towards them, with the hope that the errors would not be repeated and that those already committed would be corrected as far as possible. Two American journalists came, who tried in every possible way to make me talk and to get an interview out of me, but I eluded them, and told them to come back some other time, after I had spoken with Sforza, whom I am awaiting here. In the afternoon, among other visits, that of Col. Whitaker, with whom I had to start afresh and from every angle, on the question of the Neapolitan papers, and insist again on the need for unification for the present in a single and independent sheet.

October 28th

I had begun to read something when Duke Pietro Acquarone, Minister of the Royal Household, was announced. He had come on purpose from Brindisi, and with him I had an hour's painful conversation which resolved itself in this monotonous duet: he trying to induce me to accept 'experimentally' King Victor Emmanuel as a cohesive factor among Italian forces until the end of the war against the Germans; and I replying that the person of the King had lost all prestige, even among the popular classes, by reason of his dedication to Fascism, and could give no cohesion whatever to Italian forces, and would not even allow of the formation of a Government, that is, of a political Ministry, because the representatives of the various parties would have refused to enter a Ministry while the person of the present King remained at the head of the State. When he hinted at how much I could contribute with my word and my pen, I replied that even the greatest effort and goodwill would not have served to rekindle life in one who had willed to commit suicide. He also showed me a letter from the King of England to the King of Italy, and he told me that the Allies were imposing the retention of the King on Italy, and that there was nothing to be done against their decision. I replied that the victors can ask everything except a change of feeling in a people, everything except an injection of enthusiasm and devotion which are no longer felt. He added that the Allies any way were postponing the institutional question of a monarchy or of a republic until after the war; but I reminded him that the question to-day is one of persons and that the monarchy might presently not be discussed, if a regency were created. He also read to me signatures received, under the date of October 21st, of representatives of the various parties in Rome who would seem to accept the idea of postponing the institutional question to the end of the war; but here too I reminded him that they had not given judgment on the person of the monarchy and that certainly they would desire the abdication of the King. Acquarone told me he had a conversation with Sforza and that, since Sforza took great account of my counsel, Acquarone had come from Brindisi to Sorrento to beg me not to reinforce Sforza's negative attitude with my own, and he hoped that I would give him at least a ray of hope. I replied that I was waiting to see Sforza but that neither he nor I would obstinately hold to a thesis before having talked and discussed it, and that we found ourselves much in the position of two doctors, observing the patient with equal zeal and with equal lack of prejudice in order to diagnose his illness, the reality of which forbids us to close our eyes or foster illusions. The conclusion of the conversation was, as I wished it to be, a non-conclusion, so that the disposition of my heart and mind remained unchanged and the same as it was when he found me, nor did I say any word which would involve me.

October 29th

Matthews, who came last night, returned this morning accompanied by three journalists from important American papers, and we had a long conversation in which I reasoned on the conviction which I have reached, which is, that it is impossible to serve the person of the King and of his son, but that the institution of the monarchy need not be abolished if a regency for the Prince of Naples, who is a minor, be instituted. After objection and counter-proposals they agreed with my view and told me that they would support it in the press and that they would make it known to the American authorities. In the afternoon, accompanied by Manley, Robert D. Murphy, the U.S. Minister and Harold McMillan, the English Minister, came to see me; the latter then told me of his connection with the English publishers who have published my works. They asked me to expound the political situation to them with reference to the monarchy; this I did. In the evening, despite difficulties due to the lack of light, I began to read Matthews' book *The Fruits of Fascism*.

October 30th

Continued reading this book. Giulio Rodino and his son came, and we spoke for a long time about the questions of the day, and Rodino too is of the opinion that the King and the Prince should abdicate. In the evening towards 5 p.m. General Pavone and Tarchiani came and brought me a copy of a document sent by Sforza to Badoglio; they told me that Sforza could not come to see me at Sorrento because he is unwell in Naples and is waiting for

Badoglio there. So I decided to go with them to Naples, where we arrived soon after 7 p.m. at the Villino Mezzacapo in Via Crispi. I had a long talk with Sforza whom I had not seen since 1937. Badoglio seems willing to assume the regency for the Prince of Naples.

October 31st

I spoke with Sforza and then with Sforza and Badoglio together. We showed him that it was desirable to induce the King to abdicate because there is no other way out. Badoglio seemed to me to be already persuaded of this; he says the King will not hear of it, and Badoglio, who is an old military man and bound by his oath, would certainly not take violent action. He referred to the long struggle he had had to wage with the King to induce him to declare war on Germany. Badoglio fears that if he withdraws and, seeing the refusals of all those who have been asked, no political Ministry can be formed, the King will begin thinking of some other military personality with whom to make a military dictatorship. Sforza and I advised him to entrust Neapolitan affairs to Rodino, and he seemed agreeable to our proposal; but I don't think he can go back on his steps, since he has sent General Basso to Naples, certainly on the King's injunction, with civil and military powers and, naturally, with the mission to defend the cause of the King. Unfortunately the affairs of the combatants' units are going badly. General Pavone has replied evasively to my question, and the Americans accuse him of having so far done nothing practical about it. I have spoken with Tomkins and I think it will end by the disbanding of these volunteer units. If that should happen, we have already discussed their substitution by some similar organization. At 3 p.m. returned to Sorrento with Omodeo and reached there at 5 p.m.

Sorrento, November 1st

Finished reading Matthews' book. A sad and empty day, like all the days in the past few months; it ended with a long air raid on Naples and intense American anti-aircraft fire; a spectacle which I watched from here tensely and with an unquiet spirit.

November 2nd

Wrote a few observations to Matthews on his book. On re-reading the *Niebelungen* find they displease me more and more, careful though I am not to let moral motives of the day penetrate my judgment.

November 3rd

Cheerful news in the evening. The air raid of the other night has brought down a wing of our house in Naples and has destroyed part of the repair work which had just been finished. Elena has moved into our flat in order to give hospitality to some of the exiles from America and refugees from Rome. Two young men, very intelligent and agreeable, arrived from Florence to enlist and fight, and have found the volunteers' unit in Naples already disbanded. It is painful to see all this youthful ardour, which is gathering here so generously, wasted.

November 4th

Three journalists came to-day, two Americans and one English; the latter, a professor of philosophy, knows my friends in Oxford. A young Army captain has arrived here after many dangerous adventures, having fled from Rome since October 13th. He told me of the many sad things he has seen and of what is happening to his regiment, which was surrounded by German guns, constrained to lay down its arms, and disband.

November 5th

Have resolved to go to Naples with Morelli to talk to Sforza. Our house has made a sad impression on me, bare as it is, without windows, a kind of cavern. Sforza, who is in a nursing home, has asked me to talk to Matthews to get him to acquaint the *New York Times* about the King and the regency.

November 8th

Achille Lauro, the well-known shipbuilder, who is co-proprietor and manager of three newspapers in Naples, came to see me. I advised him to sell back to the Bank of Naples those shares which the previous regime had made him buy, and not to busy himself any more with newspapers. He told me of several instances of Fascist policy, and among others of one which caused much scandal in England, in which Ciano had sent one of his ships, the

Ischia, to Japan, full of arms, which arms had been bought and paid for by China for unloading at Hongkong. Lauro confirmed that China had paid for the cargo with several hundred thousand pounds sterling, which had been repaid to the shipbuilder in Italian paper money at the time when the Minister Host-Venturi had pressed him to order the ship (already on its way to Hongkong) to change its route and make for an Italian port, and all this on the explicit and urgent orders of Mussolini. Lauro had refused, saying it was materially impossible to execute the order, because the telegram would soon have been known in England and in other countries, and because the ship's invoices were made out for Hongkong; he assured me that the ship had got there and that he had got documents and receipts to prove it. And so on, for he told me a lot of other things connected with the same high-placed circles.

November 9th

The Head of the English Police here in Sorrento presented himself, coming in with a certain haughtiness and with a severe look, to acquaint me with his astonishment that I, an opponent of Fascism, should have become the protector of all the Fascists in Sorrento and Capri, against whom he was taking proceedings. I replied that I had never written recommendations for any one, and as he said that the Fascists here make use of my name and say that I know them and have a good opinion of them, I begged him to give me names, and he presented me with a certain list of persons who have been denounced to him, of whom some are altogether unknown to me and whose names sounded new to me, and others whom I had known on Capri, without their having informed me or I having inquired about their political precedents, among them G., who is looking after the Villa Albertini, who was very kind to me and whom I believed to be perfectly bona fide, as he is a person whom Albertini trusts. Then I told him my feeling that, since many Italians, in order to live, out of fear, through vanity or through laziness, had accepted Fascism, it would be impossible to reduce Italy to a place in which a small number of the pure, or the alleged pure, would accuse and condemn the majority of their fellow citizens, and that therefore not only justice but indulgence and forgiveness must be brought into play. In the course of our conversation the tone of his voice lowered somewhat and in the end we agreed that he would not take account of anything said to him verbally in my name or referring to my name, and that I, if I should feel the need, would write to him, to which I added that I would not write to him unless I were really in a position to communicate definite facts which might prevent an error or injustice, and that in any case I knew very little about affairs and persons in this district, where I have lived only for a few months. He too belonged to those who shake at the very idea that two men should have brought such great ruin upon the world and should have kept men away from their professions these last four years, who do not know how or when they shall go back to them, because the ex-soldiers will find their jobs taken by others. Meanwhile, Cassandro arrived from Naples to tell me about Liberal Party affairs and make me read a resolution for the abdication of the King and for the Regency, also Flora, who will stay with us some days. After them Matthews came with Packard of the United Press; and we spoke of the King who clings obstinately to the throne, thereby harming Italy, and I expounded to them our proposal for a Regency, and gave them the notes we have prepared. In the night, about 3.30 a.m., I heard firing towards Naples, and got up and saw the flares. Elena and her husband are in Naples, also Adelina, who went there yesterday morning.

November 11th

Three journalists from Canada came to visit me (I have written their names down) to whom I had to repeat my demonstration of the necessity of the King's abdication, and other judgments of mine. It is a great trial to me to have to act as my own gramophone! Have heard that Lauro had seen Del Secolo and Omodeo before he had seen me, who gave him the same advice and literally made the same declaration as I did.

November 12th

Sprigge came to see me, whom I had not seen for five years. Formerly he was on the *Manchester Guardian,* and now represents Reuter's agency, and with him an American journalist, Stoneman, who gave me details of the horrible massacre of twenty-three peasants, men, women and three year old children, at Caiazzo, by a German lieutenant aged 20 (whose name I have written, and his birthplace, but not here). The narrator had arrived in Caiazzo the day after and was still deeply moved, and he asked me to dictate an epigraph which he wants to have carved on a stone to be set up in that village. From Sprigge I learnt that the King is working busily to keep his throne, and that the English authorities are indifferent and acquiescent. Sprigge says that the Anglo-Americans have made the armistice with the King and therefore have to negotiate with him, and that the Italians should have spoken out against him in the weeks preceding the armistice in which freedom had been regained. I explained to him that there had been no freedom then, but on the contrary, martial law, press censorship and a ban on the forming of parties and on speaking in the name of parties; and I exhorted him to be diffident of such political sophisms and hypocrisies. I told him that after the so widely advertised punishment of the Fascists in Italy, England wants to see Italy led by the man most responsible for the rise of Fascism and just now the most dangerous, the King. There is no room here for legal and diplomatic formalisms, no arrangements to be excogitated, because here one is faced by an outburst of moral indignation of public feeling, quite unsuited to compromise. These last words of mine struck him and he said to me that he would pass them on to his papers. More political visits and further stories of German atrocities.

November 13th

As I got up this morning I meditated upon what is happening to me. Worked on getting clear, firm ideas about the nature of Liberalism, purged not only of democratic-demogogic medleys which open the way to dictatorships, but purged of conservative tendencies, and set in the pure tradition of Cavour again, who was not a conservative but a radical. And here it is that I find an intruder of a Liberal tinge, but in reality Communistic or at least dictatorial, which does not dare to call itself frankly Socialist or Revolutionary-Socialist, but has adopted the name of Party of Action. I shall continue to fight it in the field of ideas, because it uneducates the mind and accustoms it to hold contradictory ideas which may have pernicious practical consequences; but it may be that weak minds and revolutionary or rather confusing minds may have the ascendancy, at least for some time, over serious, loyal and clear minds. I had succeeded without begging, and still preserving Italian dignity, in getting the American command to agree to the formation of a volunteer corps under the Italian flag. But I still don't quite know whether the Allies want this attempt to fail; they should have accepted it from Donovan but they were not pleased with it. Perhaps the King and those around him opposed it at Allied Headquarters, or perhaps the Italian general whom we designated has been inactive or incapable; the fact is that the corps was being formed and has been disbanded. I worked for a revival in Neapolitan journalism and I have succeeded in getting a new name and full independence for the only newspaper which is now allowed in Naples, edited by a man of great probity and sound beliefs, Del Secolo, whom the American P.W.B. in fact brought back to Naples from the provinces where he had retired; I have also successfully faced the revolt against this proposal of mine by the Neapolitan Committee of Liberation, who wanted to support a journalist who had served the preceding regime; but although in the end the good sense of my proposal was recognized, the matter still hangs fire. With Sforza I have resolutely supported the need for the abdication of the King and the Prince, for the establishment of a regency, and I had definitely resisted all pressure put upon me to induce me to uphold the cause of the King, who even now leans upon men and upon forces that are Fascist and impedes the formation of the volunteers' corps, fearing the Republicans, and who lessens the impetus and the vigour of the war against Germany, in which we must take part. I suspect that all this suits English policy, which wants Italy as a battlefield but wants to leave its people in a condition of inferiority and impotence, so as not to be embarrassed by Italy in the alterations to be made in Europe. So it seems to me as though I have so far failed in every political action I have undertaken, and the doubt arises again in me, which I have always had, about my political aptitude, a doubt which, as a young man and as an adult, kept me away from that kind of activity and made me dedicate myself entirely to studies. I had no illusions about having acquired such an aptitude when I became a Minister in Giolitti's government, simply by administering a public office with care and devotion, as I had already done in minor offices in the past; nor indeed by conducting the opposition of the intellectuals in Italy to Fascism, because that opposition was not directly political, but above all moral. And when after the fall of Fascism I received acclamation and requests from everywhere to save Italy, and words of encouragement and hope, I was not happy about it, indeed it made me sad; it was an indication of the weakness which had beset Italy for lack of political men, born for politics, and I kept on saying that I was simply a thinking man who was trying to do his duty in the painful conditions in which Italy found itself, and that I would go on trying to do so as far as my strength would allow, but that it was no use relying on me for a great and creative political activity, which was far removed from my natural capability. And I shall continue to do what I can even now, that my doubts seem to have been confirmed by the unfortunate results of my honest endeavours; I shall continue because I cannot do otherwise, and in any case I shall comfort myself with the saying of the greatest of my patron saints, Giambattista Vico, who, having failed in a competition for the Chair of Law in the University of Naples, thought that Providence admonished him with his failure and ordered him not to busy himself with explaining law paragraphs to the students, but to recollect himself in meditation and compose *La Scienza nuova*. After this outburst, which I have noted here, I went back to work, elucidating another essay of Blanch.

November 14th

Have written thc epigraph which I was asked for on the Caiazzo massacre.[4] The American Captain Tomkins came to see me, and we talked of the general political situation, not only in Italy but in America and England, and of war aims. Del Secolo, Morelli, Sforza and other friends came and, as we were talking of present difficulties, in order to acquaint them with my frame of mind, I read them *brevitatis causa,* the notes which I made in this diary yesterday. Sforza observed, certainly to console me, "Everything you've said has brought urgent problems to the forefront, and you have opened the road to their solution."

November 16th

Agreed with Omodeo to write two memoranda, one by him and one by me, for abroad; I have been promised that they will reach American personalities. I will write to Lipmann, whom I know personally.

November 19th

Whitaker, head of P.W.B. in Naples, came back to see me together with Jackson, who works with that office elsewhere, and asked me for an article on Italian youth for a review which they

[4] It is printed in the pamphlet: *Il Dissidio della Germania con l'Europa* (Bari, 1944) at the end.

both produce. As to the question of the Naples paper, it seems to me that there is no progress; they asked my advice, they approve it as good, and then begin all over again.

November 20th

Visit from Tomkins, who has undertaken to get my letter to Lipmann.[5] Suddenly the electric light has come back in our house after about three months. Not only is it the return of the necessary good, especially at this season of very long nights, but its return came as a joyful sign of hope and confidence, which raised my spirits for a few moments. Visit from an American military man who was very sceptical about the shortness of the war, and very pessimistic about England and America, where, according to him, judgments are no longer independent and the citizens are all tied up in bureaucracy.

November 21st

Got up early, that is before dawn, which I was able to do since the electric light has come back, worked for a few hours preparing the last volume of Blanch. But from eleven until night a large number of visitors from Naples, all friends, and among others, with Morelli, the representatives of the Liberal branch, who gave me very concrete, detailed and serious reports on the extremely grave condition of the Neapolitan population (the threat of starvation owing to the exhaustion of meagre reserves, the growing number of deaths in the hospitals from malnutrition, the lack of transport from the provinces, the complete and deliberate inactivity of trams and even of the funiculars which lead to the heights of the city; and then the conditions of the workers and what is left of the machinery and of deposits of raw materials which the Anglo-Americans won't let our workers use, allowing them to be destroyed or taking them themselves, etc.); and we discussed measures to be adopted to lessen these evils. Authoritative persons in Naples who have arrived here are worried about the arrest of the director of the Bank of Naples, Frignani (put there by Fascism, but who seems to have administered affairs most correctly despite the difficult times), and fear that this arrest, made for political reasons, will be interpreted in a different way and cause panic in an institution which has 800,000 depositors and still enjoys general confidence. Have warned Spingarn, who

[5] Vol. cit.; *Per la nuova vita dell'Italia,* pp. 25–9.

belongs to the secret police, of this danger. Exchanged ideas with Sforza, Tarchiani, Del Secolo and Bergami about how to obtain the King's abdication. Another friend came, who asked me what attitude to take towards the ministry set up by the King and whether he should collaborate with it, as he has been asked to do, and as some are inclined to do, more especially as the rumour has been put about that I would be favourable to such a course. I replied by instilling a refusal and the most rigorous intransigence. Military news these days is not good either, for the Fifth Army has met with reverses in the region of Cassino and has lost Mignano and other positions again. It is said that the attempt to reach Rome will probably be abandoned, and that positions will be taken up on the line of the Garigliano during the winter.

November 26th

I had started again on the article on Italian youth, promised to Jackson, for which the difficulty lies in trying to contain it within a thousand words or a little over,[6] when Omodeo arrived, most indignant and upset about the political situation in Naples and about the inertia among some of our people, and full of anxiety lest we lose our good opportunities for lack of energy and end as the so-called 'Aventine' parties ended. Then he expounded his plan, which is to hold a meeting in the University the day after to-morrow, intended to honour me, but of a political character, in which I, Sforza and he himself should demonstrate our attitude against an interview conceded by Badoglio, which is really not in conformity with the sentiments which he had shown to Sforza and to me. I immediately accepted, putting myself at his disposal, and I had the pleasure of seeing my friend in a more serene frame of mind. But as for Badoglio I told Omodeo that while confuting him I would be polite towards him because I believe that he lies between the anvil and the hammer, not being able frankly to oppose the King, and that, in any case, we must spare him because it would not be easy to find another figure more suitable than himself to take the office of regent, according to Sforza's plan. Other friends came from Naples to interest me in the overseas exhibition grounds, whence Fascists are continually stealing materials; finally, in the evening,

[6] See *Per la nuova vita dell'Italia*, pp. 40–3.

B*

was able to finish the article which had been interrupted several times.

Left for Naples this morning with Parente and Cassandro, went to the university to make arrangements with Omodeo for to-day's proceedings and asked him to cut the second part of his speech of welcome and introduction, which refers to me and is too violent and would make my speech, which is staid and severe in its ideas and judgments, but calm and courteous, seem feeble. The second part of his speech would go well at the very end of the ceremony, together with a climax from me to Sforza and from Sforza to him. After lunching in Morelli's house, went to the university where, in the courtyard once called San Marcellino (Oh, what memories of fifty years ago when I was in the governing council of the Royal Education Committee and had to watch over the studies of the girl students of San Marcellino!), many distinguished persons were gathered, but also a good number of extremists and Communists who, whenever my speech drew a distinction between the person of the King and the institution of the monarchy, and a regency was proposed, interrupted with a prearranged concerted cry, "Down with the monarchy! Away with all the Savoys! Republic, Republic!" At certain points I had to stop talking, being smothered by the shouts; but I always started again with a clear voice, beginning with the words which had been smothered and even saying three times, "I repeat!" Thus the speech was made and heard in its entirety. I felt I was back in the Senate when I used to speak against conciliation with the Church and a senatorial rabble in one corner and a certain journalistic rabble from the press gallery used to interrupt me with inappropriate invectives, and I would let them have their say, and would repeat my sentence till I'd won and they resigned themselves to letting me go on, without disturbing me any more, till I'd finished. Among the cries there was no lack of the word *Re-pub-li-ca* scanned just in the same way as the words Du-ce, Du-ce, possibly on account of the education received in that school, and yet the interruptions did not entirely displease me because opposite me were sitting English and American journalists, and among them Sprigge, and they had been surprised that I had so obstinately maintained that the King and the Prince must go, and now they began to realize that I was a moderate on this question.[7]

[7] The Abdication Speech is in vol. cit., pp. 26–9.

November 29th

A visit from Corbino who has accepted a post in the King's Ministry and I spoke to him so pressingly and warmly about the error of accepting it (notwithstanding that he hopes to increase the bread ration for the people), that I think I have somewhat shaken him. In a number of the *Gazzetta di Bari,* given to me last night, I find a list of heavy penalties against guilty Fascists, but a provision at the end says that if they take part in the war against the Germans they will thus have purged their past, and the sanctions which have been announced will not be applied to them. Went to the Neapolitan Liberal Party branch office and then to a meeting in Morelli's house to discuss what we shall do to further the abdication of the King. Reports were made in the opposite sense; but at a certain moment I let the discussion go on and went back to Sorrento to take two of my daughters back before nightfall, and Signora Omodeo, who was going back to Positano.

November 30th

Return of moral rather than physical tiredness through not being able as yet to see a ray of hope in all our efforts, so great are the difficulties and perils of the situation. This does not lead to the conclusion that our line of action should be changed, since there is no other, and any other seemed and still seems repellent to our conscience and to any political foresight. This is one of the cases in which in order to save the future one must even be prepared to lose in the present, but never to give way, because to give way opens the way to complete and lasting corruption in Italian life.

December 2nd

Waited yesterday and to-day for a friend from Naples who should bring me information about how things are going, but no one came. This morning I thought how practically no one now talks of Mussolini, not even to rant against him. The very rumour which occasionally goes about, that he is dead, proves that he is really dead in everybody's mind. Even I seldom find feelings rising up in me against him at the thought of the ruin to which he has brought Italy and the profound corruption which he has left in every branch of public life, even in the army and among the carabinieri. And nothing would induce me to write about his person either to-day or, when I transfer myself in imagination into calmer times and brighter hopes, in the future. And yet sometimes I reflect that it may well happen and indeed is most likely to happen that my colleagues who write history (I know them well and I know how their minds work) will set about discovering bright and generous traits in that man, will even undertake his defence, his *Rettung*, his rehabilitation as it is called, and will even perhaps extol him. This I mentally address to them, almost speak to them over in that future world, which will be theirs, to warn them to let well alone, in this case to resist the temptation of paradoxical, ingenious and 'brilliant' theses, because the man really had a limited intelligence, correlated with his profound lack of moral sensibility; he was ignorant with that essential ignorance of not understanding and not knowing the elementary relations in human and civilized life; he was incapable of self-criticism, lacking scruples of conscience, he was most vain and without taste in his every word and gesture, now greedy, now arrogant. But if he were called to the Bar to answer for the damage he has done to Italy and the disgrace he has brought upon her by his words, his actions and all his superficial and corrupt arts, he might answer Italians as that disastrous leader of the people in Florence answered his comrades in exile when they reproved him for having led them to the disaster at Montaperti (as Giovanni Villani tells us), "And you, why did you believe in me?" The only problem worthy of inquiry and of meditation does not concern his personality, which is null, but Italian and European history, in which the trend of ideas and sentiments crowned the fortunes of such a man. When the German wireless announced his liberation and his return to political activity I felt indifferent, because he seemed to me a cardboard figure which has lost its wooden framework and hangs limp and folds up floppily.

December 4th

I see from the only little paper which may be printed in Naples that one may now openly write against the King and in favour of his departure, although, as is proper, articles of the opposite opinion, written by devotees of the King and the Prince, by obscure men who write in a childish way, are also accepted. As for me, I am ever more persuaded that the idea of the regency is wise, also because a republic has already been proclaimed by the Nazi-Fascists and we, by declaring ourselves republican, would find ourselves on the same ground with them, whereas the monarchic form, provisionally preserved, differentiates us completely, for it postpones the question of a monarchy or a republic until the whole Italian people has decided it in a legally correct way, i.e. by means of a constituent assembly, or rather a plebiscite.

December 5th

From 11 a.m. to 1 p.m. visits of friends from Naples on various political matters. A friend of Nitti's, Vito Reale, also came with Del Secolo. Reale is one of the under-secretaries or deputy Ministers who accepted the King's invitation and entered the Ministry. In so doing he revealed his reasons and those of his colleagues, which were to get the necessary supplies for the population and to bring some Italian divisions into the line against the Germans. Therefore they asked us, who opposed the King and his continuance as head of the State, for a truce of a couple of months. I replied that it would be impossible to comply with this truce, that it would be contrary to our feelings and unreasonable, in view of the action we have undertaken, and would make it seem as though the King had won, thus gaining advantages over us, and through our accommodation we would lose what strength we possess, which we want to use for the essential purpose of renewing Italian public life, eliminating the fascisticized King and therefore Fascism itself. Reale said that at the first sign of reactionary policy by the King, he and his colleagues would hand in their resignations; I said I would remember this and that our actions would assist in strengthening theirs *vis-à-vis* the King, whenever their intentions were good, and that, although politically divergent, in this matter we would practically converge. Then we spoke of the Italian divisions which are ready, or rather half-ready, because they have only had seven hours firing practice; the Anglo-Americans expect twenty hours, but no one knows how to get enough ammunition. Badoglio told me that there are well-armed divisions of ours in Sardinia, among them three alpine units, excellently suited for instructing the Anglo-Americans in mountain warfare. I am afraid the Anglo-Americans are purposely placing obstacles in the way of Italy's entry into the actual war, in order to have a free hand afterwards at the Peace Conference. I don't even know whether a Sforza ministry would succeed in altering this proposition, but it would try, and have certain means which the present pseudo non-political Ministry does not possess. Perhaps this is why the Anglo-Americans are interested in temporarily keeping a

King as weak as this one and with the kind of character the present King has.

December 7th

Another under-secretary came with Del Secolo, Cuomo, whom I had not seen since I had been a Minister and who has always remained an anti-Fascist. With him we spoke all over again of the things discussed with Reale. In the evening Omodeo came to talk of Neapolitan affairs and of his relations, as Rector of the University, with the Allied authorities, towards whom he has taken up a dignified and resolute stand. I advised him to take part in the Committee of Liberation and, although he states in public and in private that he fully agrees with my restatements of the idea of liberty and of Liberalism, he does not want to join the Liberal Party by reason of quite personal antipathies towards some of its members, so I encouraged him to join the so-called 'Party of Action' (to which he seems more inclined, although he criticized and refuted it in the past); he could thus perhaps take the place of the present representative of that Party inside the Committee of Liberation who is very weak.

December 8th

A young American naval officer of Italian origin, with parents in Campobasso, who has studied philosophy and music and had heard my name several times from his teacher of philosophy, who said he knew me personally in England, came to see me and asked me to sign a copy of *Estetica,* which he had bought in Naples. His name is Olindo Martello. Every day one or more officers, non-commissioned officers, American soldiers, and (more seldom) English soldiers, whom my daughters have met either at gatherings here or at the houses of friends, come to my house. They come to talk with my daughters, often to read English books or to practice conversation. They are good people, simple and human; I approve their coming to our house because I know what it means for them, being far from their families, to find themselves in a family atmosphere. The other day I was called from my room by the sound of Sylvia sobbing near the front door. I found her standing face to face with a young soldier who seemed lost and did not understand why she cried so much. Finally, I understood that he was an acquaintance of the previous week who had gone to the front line.

Sylvia had asked an officer who had come from the front for news of him and he had replied, "He was a good soldier but he had just been killed," which had caused her great grief. Now, seeing him safe and sound (the officer's news had evidently arisen from a mistake in names) she had been so deeply moved that she had broken into uncontrollable tears. I am less pleased (though I say to myself that one cannot continually suppress the young) to find that they seem unable to avoid invitations to parties, teas and dances in the hotels where they are staying; invitations which they cannot always refuse and which should be received courteously, but which I would like to see accepted very seldom, especially as many Fascists or former Fascist families go there or at least try to get invited. Even some young German ladies here long to get the invitations! In the afternoon I took a rest from my lengthy labours, correcting and rewriting Blanch's essays—that Neapolitan whose mind was devoted to duty and who was constantly trying to touch every part of public and political life with the light of truth—and steeped myself in poetry, in ancient Italian poetry, rereading the lines in an anthology collected with much taste and containing the fine translations of my German friend, Hans Feist, published (under the pseudonym of Hans Frederick) in Switzerland, where he had taken refuge from racial persecution. This was one of the last books that arrived by post in Naples, and Alda had found it there and brought it to me. Heard two talks on the wireless to-night, one by Parente on the Liberal Party, very accurate and lucid, which I listened to with pleasure because the truth is always pleasant to hear, and the other by Professor Antonino Pane, on the Party of Action, very vague and inaccurate (he said among other things that it was a 'Mazzinian' Party, and that therefore it had adopted the motto 'Action,' whereas Mazzini used the phrase "Thought and action," and here the thought is lacking), and very muddled, because he barely touched on the programme which that Party has formulated and which would have amazed most of his hearers.

December 9th

Col. T. came to see me to tell me about the fairly divided views in military circles regarding the King and our request that he should abdicate, and how varied the views are. He said that those who understand the question are for the Regency, and that the army, especially in north and central Italy (whence he came in October), has a strong aversion for the person of the King. He asked me to set down briefly an exposition of the question in a letter which he might use, and which would support what he had told me; and I wrote it.

December 10th

Carlo Sforza came with his son and let me read some documents which he had written and left copies of them with me, and I gave him a few pages of mine for him to use as occasion arises. We discussed the possibility, which now seems to be arising, of an abdication by the King in favour of his son and we came to the conclusion that, despite pressure put on us by our friends and various good people, it was necessary for us to maintain our firmness, also because we must not let our faithful friends in Rome and in northern Italy find themselves up against a political situation which has been compromised by us.

December 11th

Talked with a man in the Foreign Office who had come from Brindisi, is a son of an admiral and was introduced to me by Elena, who knew him; he said that in Brindisi people say that I have been converted to the Republic by Sforza and that the Regency is a 'trick' on our part by which to get rid of the monarchists. I replied that, if anything, it was I who had encouraged Sforza in this direction, he being unaware of the latest development, since the Allies had rapidly taken him to Brindisi, without even allowing him to halt in Naples; I had sent him warning advice in a letter, in which I had outlined my doubts and my judgment on the policy undertaken by the King after July 25th. As to the 'trick,' I said we were not Fascists and there were certain things we did not do, that the Regency was serious and would be defended loyally, even though its future could not be assured since it would not depend on us, but on the whole people. He repeated the old story: that the King will not go away, that we were wasting our breath, and that therefore it would be better to compromise. I replied that we would not compromise, because we are certain that we see things in a just light and feel that we have a moral justification on our side, and that we will go on hammering away and use every means we can possibly think of, whenever occasion shall offer, and we shall see with what result. Articles and pamphlets by the King's defenders are pretty poor stuff compared with our reasoned polemics.

December 12th

Sforza replies, refuting the interpretation given to a letter written by him to Badoglio before he returned to Italy. Also there are silly references to my 'ambition.' Would to heaven I had some, because then I would have a vitality which I have not had in these matters, even in my earliest years. A few weeks ago I was listening to a speech of Sforza's in English to some thirty American journalists in the course of which he said that neither he nor I had ambitions, and when I saw that one of the journalists whom I knew was taking notes, I asked him for his note-book, and I added this comment thus on Sforza's words: "I have no ambitions, but seventy-eight years."[8] On the other hand, have agreed with the Committee of Liberation that it should pass a vote, greeting with joy and fervour the first flags of the Italian soldiers advancing against the Germans on whom our Italian eyes are fixed, regardless of what political party we belong to.

December 14th

In the evening Naples wireless gave a reply of mine to Badoglio, of which I had given a copy to Morelli and to Omodeo:[9] it sounded severe to me, almost painful, but I recognised it as just and necessary.

December 15th

Could not sleep for some hours between 2 and 5 o'clock, my thoughts continually fixed on how everything which generations of Italians have built up during this last century, politically, economically and morally, has been irremediably destroyed. Ideal forces with which we must face the difficult future without looking back, suppressing our regrets, survive only in our hearts. In the afternoon Elena told me that some ladies of the British Red Cross, accompanied by an officer, came to visit the villa in which we are living and that they covered it with many of their cries of 'beautiful!' and were talking among themselves about requisitioning it as a Red Cross club. Since my daughter had not received reassuring replies, and knowing myself how obstinate and wilful women can be, I asked the American Governor of Vico Equense, who is a naval Lieutenant-Colonel, a magistrate by profession, a Mr. Musmanno

[8] Croce wrote this in English. Tr.
[9] *Per la nuova vita dell'Italia*, pp. 30–1.

of Italian origin, to be so good as to come and see me for a moment. He kindly came at once and, having heard what the trouble was, he sent me a notice to put up at the entrance to my house forbidding any requisitioning for the moment, pending a permanent order which he would get after communicating with the authorities in Naples. A great number of Italian and foreign political figures come to this villa in which I live, and are put up as far as space allows; moreover, I have brought several thousand rare volumes here which I would not know where or how to transport.

December 16th

Colonel Whitaker, on sick leave from the front at Cassino and now resting here in Sorrento, came to lunch. He told me of German prisoners who are convinced that Germany has lost the war, but who do not think they should fight any the less, nor do they have any regrets about the horrors they have committed because 'they were obeying orders.' He also told me that the American soldiers are behaving courageously but are not inspired by the ideal of liberty, nor do they feel it as a motive for fighting the Germans. I replied that for my part I have reached the conviction that this is not a war for liberty but for independence, for dominion and for political and economical advantage, just like all other wars, and that the war for liberty will have to be fought later on, not with arms but with much more varied and suitable means.

December 17th

Sforza came with Caracciolo to tell me that I must go to Naples, because Allied authorities had forbidden the congress of the southern Committees of Liberation,[10] and that therefore they had thought of sending a protest to Roosevelt, Churchill and Stalin based on the deliberations of the new Moscow Agreement in which Italy is assured the right of free speech and free assembly. At the Committee of Liberation meeting, over which I presided, I got them to vote on the protest, despite the opposition of the Catholic party, whose representatives are, as usual, too circumspect and cautious and to whom I ended by saying, that if they would not sign we would do without them, but that such a refusal would be the beginning of a break-away by their party from the union of the parties, because this time it was a question of defending the liberty of all parties. However,

[10] For an account of this, see vol. cit., pp. 35–9.

just as we were going out for the appointment we had fixed with the American authorities, one of the two Catholic representatives told me that the other had gone to ask advice from one of their leading figures (I think from Giulio Rodinò), and that probably they would decide to sign; this they did and joined us later at the Command Headquarters. The American authorities were extremely affable and could not find any logical reason why the Congress should have been forbidden and said that they knew nothing of a ban on the Commemoration of Amendola, which had been arranged and allowed for Sunday next, but which had been forbidden to-day. So they asked Arangio Ruiz, who had received the permission and then had it revoked, to come back at 11 a.m. to-morrow so that they could look into the matter. [The following day permission was granted again, the revocation was revoked and the Commemoration was held with many thousands of people present, a speech by Cianca, another by Sforza and a vote on an anti-Fascist Order of the Day, which included the King among the Fascists.] I believe that the agents whom the King sends to Naples (among whom I am told is Naldi, at the head of propaganda) have given false references and have roused the suspicions of the American authorities. As to the Congress of Committee representatives, I think that if we had insisted the ban would also have been lifted, but since there was little promise in a Congress so hurriedly summoned, I was much more concerned with the protest we presented and the fact that the aforesaid authorities promised to telegraph it to Algiers (and this they did and the English wireless mentioned our protest in the news, with some explanation which confirmed the principle established at Moscow; so that our object was achieved).

December 18th

Wrote a letter to the ing. Laterza[11] in Bari with instructions about how to reconstitute the Liberal Party there.[12] The Lady Director of the National Library at Naples tells me of damage done to cases of library books by the American soldiery. These had been taken for safety to monasteries and religious houses in a region where it was thought they would be safe, but where there has been fighting, or there is fighting now. It is known that the Germans have taken away the cases of the National Library at Teano, including some of my books, but no one knows where to. I decided to write

[11] Ing. is the Italian title Ingeniere or Engineer.
[12] See vol. cit., pp. 114–15.

a letter to General Clark to ask him to lend the Directress of the National Library a couple of lorries so that they might bring back from Calvi Risorta to Naples those cases of books which are there. Conversation with Sprigge and with another journalist from Reuters whom I enlightened, with much energy but calmly, on the realities of the Italian political situation.

December 20th

Letter from an old German professor who taught in Naples for about half a century, and who writes of his people in a thoughtful, serious way. Two journalists, Stoneman of the *Chicago News* and another of the *News Chronicle* of London, have been asked in telegrams from their papers to get an Appeal to the Peoples of the Allied Nations from me, which I had to restrict to a little more than 200 words.

December 21st

My friend Omodeo, whose intelligence and moral integrity I greatly esteem, torments me with his suspicions and diffidence which prods this way and that, and recently into all my friends and collaborators in the Liberal Party. I see that he thinks I am too trusting and that I let myself be used; which proves how one's friends often misunderstand their friends. I am the most diffident of men because I am extremely diffident of myself and continually subject my ideas, my judgments and my actions to self-criticism; but I do not shut myself away from others in a suspicious diffidence which can be likened to fear, because then I would simply be weaving imaginary webs. Moreover, whenever people have tried to take me in, my reactions have been violent, and it has never happened to me yet to make friends again with any one who has given proof of insincerity. Del Secolo came with three members of the Basilicata Committee of Liberation, who are determined that we should pass from arguments, spoken or printed, to some other form of practical activity, and have outlined proposals of which I shall speak with Sforza.

December 24th

Matthews is going home to see his people in Mexico and counts on coming back early in March, because he does not think, unless something unexpected happens, that Rome can be occupied before then. He brought me an epilogue for his book on the history of

Fascism which Elena is translating. Many other visits from foreigners and Italians connected with the coming festival. Staying with us are Sforza and his son, Tarchiani and Caracciolo di Castanietto. I am told that I shall shortly be visited by ex-Minister Piccardi, now an officer in the units which Badoglio and Marshall Messe have formed, and that he will want an appeal to the soldiers from me, for they are very depressed. The King has contributed about six thousand soldiers who are camping in and around Avellino, and fourteen hundred of these were ordered by the American General to capture the heights of Monte Lungo. They bravely went into the assault and accomplished the difficult operation, but were unable to resist a heavily armoured German counter-attack, in which they lost five hundred killed while the others withdrew, having lost confidence and spreading insecurity among the remainder. The local population greeted them with the complaint, "Why do you let yourselves be killed for the King?" The position was then retaken after a lengthy bombardment by American artillery and with the Italian units taking part. Now they have all been withdrawn from the front for reorganization, but I don't know whether this will be successful, because it seems that there have also been many desertions. I recalled the volunteer corps which we had obtained permission to form in October and which fell through for reasons which are still obscure to me, possibly reasons of a different order, but not unconnected. Without doubt, certain zealous agents of the monarchy were mixed up in it and I met them, and much false news was spread about it. I remembered an American officer who spoke to me on October 31st about the necessity for disbanding the early volunteer formations, saying that a corps of 500 volunteers from the King's side had arrived and were ready, very well equipped and armed, and he had asked me what I had thought should be done with them. I had answered, "Accept them at once and send them to fight. If we fail in our own attempt, we must make room for those who are ready to fight the Germans, wherever they come from." But of this volunteer corps I was never able to establish the truth, and I received contradictory news about it, even the news that it had never existed.

December 25th

On getting up this morning Sforza was enchanted with the spectacle of the Gulf of Naples seen from Sorrento and from the villa in which I live. I myself am tempted by the enchantment when I look from the balconies of my study, but then a kind of remorse draws me away from its spell and the temporary relaxation, for I feel it to be sinful and illicit amid the tragedy of Italy and of the world. (Sometimes I am reminded of the verses in that poem to Sorrento by the fifteenth century humanist, Pietro Gravina, whose life I wrote, the poem which begins:

"Naturae gaudentis opus, dulcissima tellus . . .")

Sforza has been to a meeting in a theatre and they tell me he made a fine speech, which was liked. I did not go, however, but I advised him to keep to generalities so as to avoid getting his name mixed up in local controversy; friends had warned me to make sure of telling him to beware of the many invitations which he gets from little provincial towns, and I did so on the occasion of this new speech. As a joke I drew his attention to some lines in Shakespeare's *Henry IV*, which I had open, in which the King advised his son, who was then the friend of Falstaff, but was to become Henry V, how he should behave when preparing to take the throne over from his weak predecessor, presenting himself

"Like a robe pontifical, never seen but considered at."

December 26th

In these days I have continually had to repeat (and Sforza, when I asked him, agreed with my view) that the regency, if we get it, will be a serious affair to us who proposed it. Personally we are bound to defend it with all our strength, because we would not know how, nor indeed would we intend, to play the famous part of Don Liborio Romano in 1806, Minister to Francis II, who persuaded the King to rejoin his army on the Volturno and, when the King had done so, opened the gates of Naples to Garibaldi and became the Minister of the Lieutenant-Generalcy (even though Don Liborio had serious concern for public security in what he did). Now, at the end of the year, reviewing what has happened, I find some positive result from our work, because firstly, we have made a public political reckoning with the person of the King, and his only defences have been pamphlets and articles, stupid ones and often ungrammatical; secondly, we have pointed a way out in our proposal for a regency; thirdly, our discussions have provided Italy once again with a political opposition, which has been lacking these last twenty years and which has already made its efficacy felt since the government has been forced to adopt certain measures. The rest of Italy will come upon this state of affairs, and we believe that these things will be accepted and will be brought a stage further when we shall be suddenly reunited. For my part I have tried to keep a certain moderation in everything that has been said and done and attempted, for I have learnt as a young man from Francesco de Sanctis how moderation can be "a terrible weapon, which men hardly know, otherwise they would use it more often." I have avoided the frequent use of the word 'republic,' fearful lest the country so newly free of a dictatorship might fall under a new dictatorship, by means of a republic lacking in tradition and preparation. A colonel from the Abruzzo (who is a lawyer in Rome), Sig. Carlo Sandirocco, has told me and my friends horrible things which the Germans are doing in the Abbruzzi region: massacres violations, burnings of houses and whole villages, looting of everything that can be taken away, destruction of the rest, etc.; things which I hardly dare write down and dare not repeat to myself.

December 27th

In the afternoon two officers from the American Political Service came to see me, sent by Spingarn, for information about a lady who lives here and of whom I know nothing; but one of the two inquisitors wanted my signature on the flyleaf of a little volume which he had in his pocket, and I saw that it was in Greek, and he told me that he was a student at Harvard University. Have in mind a pamphlet for publication with the title *Germany's Dissent from Europe,*[13] and mentally I have woven the pattern of the introduction.

December 28th–29th

Written and revised this pamphlet. Reread a few pages of old writings of mine and especially of *Conversazioni Critiche,* and I wondered why people have asked me several times to occupy a University Chair, when I had already made my own Chair in the heart of Italy by answering questions and giving explanations (which now take the form of *quaestiones* and *objectiones*), in this and in other volumes, enjoying a much larger and more varied public than I could have had in lecture rooms filled with students about to take degrees. Flora and Morelli came. Shall go to Naples to-morrow with the latter on various matters, and for a meeting which he has

[13] Written then, published in early 1944 (Bari, Laterza).

arranged with Enrico de Nicola, who was the last freely elected President of the Italian Chamber.

December 30th

In Naples, having heard that all the bank safes are sealed and may not be opened unless an American officer has reviewed their contents, I went to the Bank of Italy to see Colonel Nelson, who met my objections by saying that the ruling had been made because it was said that there were Fascist political documents in the safes, and that in fact a few had been found already, "fairly useful ones for our common enterprise," he said to me. Thus I got the two safes open which I have in two banks and I reacquired the free use of them; in one of them were some very rare books which I found again with pleasure. Then I went to Morelli's house, where I was to meet De Nicola. Later Sforza came to our meeting. De Nicola said he was fully in agreement with us on the points about the King and the Prince of Piedmont withdrawing in some way or another, but he produced some doubts about the regency we propose (the regent or one of the regents later on might renew a Fascist dictatorship, etc.). These were not so much objections as warnings of dangers such as accompany every human action and undertaking, and against which there is no other defence but intelligence, vigilance and the people's determined will, or rather that of the governing and responsible class. Instead he proposed a Lieutenant-Generalcy, lasting two or three years, that is, until the people can be consulted and give its reply upon what institutional form it prefers. I asked, "Whose Lieutenant-Generalcy?" Obviously, the King's, who would nominate the holder and run the Institution to his own end; thus that very evil which could and might well exist, but not irremediably, in the kind of regency we Liberals suggest, would be institutionally inherent in the Lieutenant-Generalcy. I drew his attention to the fact that his proposal seemed more harmful to the monarchical institution than ours, since it cuts at the very roots, by preventing the birth of a constitutional monarchy out of those roots, in the shape of a prince educated by the new anti-Fascist and Liberal Italy, and that it would logically lead to a republic, since if all continuity is taken from the institution of the monarchy the vote of the people or a legislative chamber or constituent assembly would be most unlikely to go back to the monarchy; the King would probably object to it more than to an abdication, which he has turned down. But De Nicola, as though more intuitive about the King's character, replied, "He will oppose the abdication, but you'll see, he will accept the Lieutenant-Generalcy." We asked him whether he had any candidate for the Lieutenant-Generalcy; but this search and designation of a suitable person seemed to him a question to postpone to a later period. De Nicola, with his ratiocinative and subtle cleverness, spoiled his own proposal in the end by saying that it was simply an idea for consideration and that he was not tied to it nor intended making it public in opposition to our idea. Then I said to him that during the whole Fascist period I had very rarely seen him and, though always very friendly with him, we had never talked of politics—that in one way or another he should now enter the political arena, as a most important deputy for a long time and as one-time President of the Chamber; he should not leave the arena to me and Sforza, for I am a man of studies, political *malgré moi*, and if he joined us I would be able to follow my keenest desire and step back, pushing him in front of me. But he remained deaf to this proposal. The conversation left me with the impression that he is as contrary as we are to the King's remaining, and to the Prince; and that it is mere hearsay, put about in the last few days by people who don't know him, that he is the head of an Italian Monarchist Party (that same Party which prints those foolish and ungrammatical pamphlets here in Naples, to which I have already referred). Towards 3.30 p.m. I had to leave De Nicola and Sforza talking and go back to Sorrento.

December 31st

Had to talk to Omodeo about the contradiction into which he has fallen as Rector of the University by opening a political club as a section of the Party of so-called Action, giving it a programme which is substantially mine, to which he has always agreed and been faithful, a programme which is, taken all in all, a criticism of the programme of the Party of Action (in which criticism he has always been, and even now says he is, in full agreement with me). He answered that he intends leading the young people along the lines of this rigorous programme and, if the Party of Action disowns his work, he will leave the Party and produce a crisis. I explained that this seemed to me a long and roundabout course and that it would be simpler to initiate a revision of the programme of the Action Party, since it has been published without ever having been submitted to the discussion of members, who in the first place were simply an anti-Fascist concentration intent on liberty and to which I also belonged. It had been written, I know not by whom, and illicitly published by an anonymous decision. Only after such a revision of the programme could the question of this party be solved, and perhaps then the Socialist or indeed the Communist element in it would move towards the Social-Communist parties and the Liberals towards Liberalism; for the whole question is one of method and he who wants the method of discussion, elections, assemblies and majority votes and does not want dictatorship in any form, either tenuous or mild, is a Liberal. He who follows the opposite method and talks of making "an economic revolution, after which true liberty shall be set up," does not know what liberty is and tends towards dictatorship, be it Fascist or Communist.

January 1st, 1944

Raimondo and Elena and Flora went away again. A little later a car came to fetch Lydia and Sylvia to take them to the opening of the San Carlo (*Lucia di Lammamoor*) to which they were invited. Alda wanted to stay behind with us. Finished the revision of the current number of the *Critica*. Visitors, but in smaller numbers. In the evening Captain Sylvester, otherwise known as Max Salvadori, brought our two daughters back and spent the evening with us.

January 2nd

Took a brief walk and began wondering how and whether I can go on with the *Critica* in the coming year, because I am engaged in writing pamphlets and political or semi-political articles which I have to publish elsewhere because of their urgency and actuality. They are unsuitable for the *Critica*, which has also lost touch with its readers, there being no way now of distributing the numbers. They accumulate in the storeroom of Laterza, pending future events. In 1944 I could carry on with mainly literary articles, which are largely ready. And then? Should it not placidly pass out? Or should it be changed to conform with new conditions? And how?

January 3rd

Sforza and Morelli came to talk over the conversations with De Nicola and to tell me how he seems disposed to intervene publicly along with us; first he wants to see the King and tell him energetically that there is no other solution than that which he has excogitated : the Lieutenant-Generalcy. If the King does not accept he will explain his idea in public and make common cause with us. For the reasons already given, I doubt whether the King will accept; but if he accepts, since the Prince who should have received the crown cannot lower himself to a mere Lieutenant-General, and since the office cannot be given to any one already compromised by Fascism (like the Duke of Aosta, King of Croatia), there would only be the Count of Turin, the only one who behaved with dignity and kept away from Fascism. But he is old, deaf and mentally incapable, so much so that he used to say he was "the imbecile of the family." Whatever happens we shall see what will come of it. Morelli told me about Neapolitan matters and among other things about the sequestration of our pamphlets by the Italian or Royal police, at the request, so Morelli says, of the Allied authorities. Parente immediately protested to them and I also, with a letter to Colonel Hume in which I spoke of various town matters, among them the question of the newspapers. I was dozing off when the town major of Sorrento arrived, together with another officer, to tell me that the villa we live in has been requisitioned as a rest camp for forty Red Cross nurses who are in Naples. I gave all the reasons and defensive arguments I could, without succeeding in getting them to leave me alone to work here, and not only me.

January 4th

The way ordinary and private annoyances, great and small, intrude into the tragedy of the nation and of civilization! The feeling that I have not sufficient time before me to work at the cause which is dear to me and see it triumph—all this exasperates me to the point of thinking of the quiet peace which death, or the promise of death, affords. Fortunately, however, I seem to have an inexhaustable supply of comfort and of renewed serenity which relieves me of miseries and, together with my private dignity, gives me back the necessary strength. And I repeat Faust's words which I learnt by heart as a young man, "Erquickung hast du nicht gewonnen wenn sie dir nicht aus eigner Seele quillt." This I repeated this morning as I went into my study, the very room which was threatened yesterday and which I shall have to defend. Wrote a note to add to my critical essay on Blanch, a note about the concept of 'foresight' in connection with political duty. A young engineering student from Bologna, who succeeded in escaping from a German round-up of young men in Florence, came to see me. He had reached Bari, where he had enlisted and had fought in the Royal Militia near Cassino. He spoke with great seriousness and the stress of sincerity in describing his state of mind and that of some of the best of the young Italians, who are not at all ignorant or at sea politically. He himself is tormented by doubt, but meanwhile he has given his word of honour as a King's volunteer; he does not believe in the efficacy of the militia, several of whose officers have proved their incapacity (a colonel has had to be removed, with shocking results for the soldiers, who believe they are badly led by their superiors). He has another specific undertaking in mind with a view to liberating Italy from the Germans. I have sent him to Sforza and to other friends in Naples. More visitors and among them the widow of Berneri, who was the scapegoat, indeed the only one to be condemned for an action conceived by Roselli and other exiles in Paris, to be undertaken in Italy with explosives, and who afterwards went to fight in Spain, and was shot in Barcelona, not by Franco-ists but by Russian Communists who accused him of being a Republican democrat. In the evening Musmanno came. I have entrusted him with looking after my continued stay here. I told him I did not want to turn to General Clark, whom I have already asked to rescue a large part of the books in the National Library and who immediately met my request and sent Colonel Hume here to me; but that time I was fighting for a strictly public interest, while now it is a question of a private or seemingly private interest.

January 5th

End of alarums about requisitioning. Musmanno has been busy and has gone to the Town Major. He tells me that the latter acted on higher orders and that the lady who wanted the house or started the business, and whom I have never seen, had assured the Allied authorities that she had already come to an agreement with me! He says I am not to worry because the house will not be touched. He came back in the evening and told me that a British brigadier had come to Sorrento and had insisted upon immediate requisitioning, but that he had explained my reasons energetically and with sound arguments. The General said, "Let us put the Senator in another suitable villa." Reply, "Why don't you go there, and so avoid a double removal." The General, "It is a question of what we want above all." Reply, "But in this you show a lack of respect for Senator Croce, who etc., etc." The General, "Up to the present the Italians have not suffered as much as the English." Reply, "Even if they have not suffered as much as you, this would give the German Fascist wireless in Rome a fine opportunity to bemoan the ungracious manner in which you treat a man who has always upheld the Liberal ideal, etc., etc." Musmanno made it clear to the General that he would oppose any requisition with all the means at his disposal, and he tapped a big pistol which bulged in his pocket the while. (A pistol, he said, which without hitting a man can knock him down merely by the force of its explosion. This roused Silvietta's enthusiasm and she begged, "Oh, please shoot, to let us see!") This Governor Musmanno is an amusing and curious person. He is of Italian origin but he does not know from what part of Italy his family emigrated. I should say Sicily or Calabria. There are people in Naples with his surname. He is both generous and brave, subtle and full of ordinary common sense, and has a gay and easy manner. He speaks of this incident as of a battle won by himself and calls it by the name of one of the first battles which the Americans won against the English in the war of Independence.

January 7th

An American called Old—really a Vecchi—came back to see me with a message from Shean, whom I knew years ago in Naples and who wants to translate my pamphlet on Germany. He also brought me a pretty obscure telegram from London about partisan operations in northern Italy. He confirms what others have told me, that in America nothing at all is known about the real situation in Italy, that Fascism enjoys great numbers (indeed the majority) of Americans among its admirers, owing to the propaganda over there and to the welcome which used to be given here to American personages, who would be covered with honours and would only be allowed to see what Fascism wanted them to see, and on their return home would praise the regime and the general happiness enjoyed by Italy. (This is correct and I have had proof of it, which I will not mention here.) He said he felt that Italy's present problems were so numerous and so difficult and dense as to induce a kind of despair in any one who considered them. As for America, he excluded the danger of Fascism there after the war, because production there was far greater than consumption and because anyway, in the great economic crisis of fifteen years ago, the American unemployed had not lowered their standard of living.

January 8th

Cassandro and Parente have come here bringing news of affairs in Naples and from what they say I feel concerned about some disagreement, practically a break, between Sforza and De Nicola, which must be overcome and repaired at once. Thus, instead of a letter for which they ask me, I said I would go to-morrow to Naples. Our objections to the sequestration of our pamphlets have been acknowledged and my proposals about the newspapers have also been favourably received. The good Musmanno, who often comes to see us and is always gay, has had me photographed in various poses in the garden standing beside him, with his pocket bulging with the famous pistol.

January 9th

An American officer has brought me a letter from Colonel Hume about newspapers. At noon Morelli came and I immediately left with him for Naples. During the crossing he gave me details of the disagreement between Sforza and De Nicola. It had been agreed that he would have tried to persuade the King to withdraw, leaving a Lieutenant-General who would be chosen from among the Princes of the Royal House, excluding the Duke of Aosta, King of Croatia and (it was implied) also the Crown Prince. De Nicola has had a visit from Badoglio, has expressed his ideas on the situation, but not on the question of a Lieutenant-General. Badoglio listened with great interest and wished him to explain these ideas to the King. De Nicola does not want to ask for an audience but wants to wait for the King to invite him. Meanwhile De Nicola has asked Sforza what to do if the King should propose giving the Lieutenant-Generalcy to his son? This possibility was already envisaged in our conversation of December 30th and we turned it down as inacceptable, not only by us but by the King himself, in that it would in certain ways diminish the position of his son. But when De Nicola proposed it again, Sforza seemed prepared to accept the situation arising from such a step, especially because of public opinion, which is growing impatient and wants a regular Government with authority for the men in it, and practically blames us for having delayed its formation up to the present. However, the following day Sforza had received news from the Liberation Committee in Rome that the abdication of the King and of the Prince, and the setting up of a Regency, were the extreme limits to which it could go. Sforza thereupon wrote to De Nicola and withdrew his previous compromise. De Nicola was indignant and declared that he would drop everything and would return to solitary retirement. This would have greatly discredited and damaged our cause and brought upon us the aggravation of having alienated a man so authoritative as De Nicola and so highly thought of by the whole of Naples. Our excessive intransigence would have been blamed for forcing him to take no more part in our political action. I invited Sforza to come to Morelli's house and he immediately recognized the justice of my arguments and allowed me to come to an agreement with De Nicola and to accept, if absolutely necessary, even a Lieutenant-Generalcy of the Prince of Piedmont, provided it was sufficiently guaranteed against a stab in the back by the King, through his son and through the people who might surround the son. I shall carry this business through with De Nicola simply in order to keep him by our side, for I have little hope of it being successful. Have seen Piccardi, who came from the camp of the King's soldiers and drew a depressing picture of the state of mind of those few thousand men who don't want to fight, and still less fight for the King. He again asked us, the opposition, to draw up an appeal to clarify the state of mind of those soldiers; but I had to confess that what he is hoping for (to get Marshall Messe to make declarations upon which we could hang our own words) does not meet with Messe's support. Messe holds that he cannot step out of his military office and engage in politics. Arangio Ruiz told me about his questioning by the Inter-Allied Committee for Italian Affairs and especially by the Russian representatives, who are concerned about the effect of the abdication of the King, of a breach between the country and the Army and the Navy, who would then have refused to fight.

January 10th

Piccardi went back this morning to Sforza and gave him new details about disintegration among the King's troops. He showed Sforza an article in a little paper of Avellino in which one of these soldiers had written that they were in no mind to fight for the King, after the way Sforza and Croce had demonstrated the weaknesses in the King's character. Sforza replied in a most dignified way, and I have asked him to put the reply in writing and have it published in his and my name, so as finally to dispel the accusations thrown at us of opposing an army which fights under the royal ensign. I then went with Morelli to fetch De Nicola at his house and I took him to Morelli's house, where he spoke cordially with Sforza and we quickly cleared the matter up and came to an agreement. In case, in the course of the conversation, the King should propose handing over the Lieutenant-Generalcy to his son, which seems to me an unlikely idea, it will be necessary to draw his attention to the damage which the cause of the monarchy would suffer by degrading his son to the rank of Lieutenant-General, when normally where the father retires the son should succeed to the throne. Also, if necessary, to accept the proposal but to add that De Nicola would refer back to us in those matters which concern us, and that then we would ask for and take the necessary guarantees.

January 11th

A visit from René Marsigli, who has the rank of Ambassador (as such he has been in Turkey) and is now a member of the Inter-Allied Committee. I had the usual conversation with him and clarified the difficulties about the effect of the abdication which is being pressed on the King. Then the other commissar arrived, the Russian one, Andrea Vishinsky, and he asked me and Sforza, who came soon after, the same questions, to which we replied fully. It did not need much effort to demonstrate to him how the King's abdication, far from dispiriting the Army and the Navy, would encourage them to fight. I don't know what goes on in the mind of this Russian who is, for our part, inscrutable. I gave him a present of a pamphlet of mine on Communism and its history. After our conversation he talked to my daughters, two of whom, having started learning Russian, lisped a few words of it to him. When he heard that they had read the poems of Serge Esenin with admiration, he observed, with the usual conventional Bolshevic judgment, that Esenin was *passé* because he sang his 'personal' sentiments, whereas the new and true Russian poetry contained 'social' ideas and sang the feelings of the proletariat and of Bolshevism. His secretary, a big young man, in talking with my daughters and looking over the fairly luxurious house (which is not ours but which we inhabit), said to them that we were evidently 'capitalists.' For freshness or sharpness of thought there is little to hope for from people of this type. The Frenchman, on the other hand, clearly told Sforza and myself that here in southern Italy the Allies were repeating the errors they had already committed in French North Africa, by supporting the Fascists but not the Liberals (in the other case they had supported the followers of Giraud and not those of de Gaulle). He regretted it, of course, but I don't know how much authority he has in the Committee, where he seems to me to be simply a figurehead. The other two members, the Englishman McMillan and the American Murphy, came to see me at the end of October.

January 12th

Del Secolo came to see me with Cuomo, who is a member of the King's Government in control of Public Instruction. We spoke of the fate of the various academies and I again proposed that the Italian Academy should be abolished, and the *Academia dei Lincei* should be restored. Del Secolo made me read a resolution against a congress just held in Bari by a so-called Liberal-Democratic party (that is Royalist) and I altered it, making it more resounding still. The American journalist, Chinigo, asked me to give at least an opinion about the shooting of Ciano, de Bono and the others,[14] and I replied that it seemed superfluous to me to say what everybody was thinking; that it was a crime added to the other crimes, and a horror. Friends in Naples have asked me for a letter setting down the criteria to be followed in the 'epuration' which is about to begin and which we Liberals wish to see conducted in the most temporary and indulgent way,[15] and I wrote it.

January 13th

A young English poet, John Gawsworth, came to see me from Manfredonia, where he is stationed, and gave me a little volume of his poems.

January 14th

The usual visits of American and British officers, whom I entertain for a few moments and then leave to talk and read with my daughters. Sforza writes, insisting that I go with him to the Congress of the Committees of Liberation to be held in Bari, where 'some-

[14] Tried, condemned and shot by Mussolini's Republican Special Tribunal in Verona. Tr.

[15] The letter can be read in *Per la nuova vita dell'Italia*, pp. 46–9.

thing may happen.' I think and hope so too, and I shall go; but something in my bones tells me this journey will be repugnant. They say it is tiring, full of incidents and accidents, and dangerous at this season and at my age, which I have to take into account now and then. I am not so frightened at the prospect of the labours of the congress as I am about the number of people whom I must see again in Bari, the many conversations after the months that I have not been in that city and after so many different events. And I would not find my old friend Laterza there any more. I think I shall end by not going and shall ask Sforza to represent me and to let me know about all the decisions that are taken and of the actions which will be decided upon.

January 15th

Further requests from various quarters that I should go to Bari, while my daughters all discourage me from embarking on the journey. Actually Raimondo, as he left here, advised me not to risk the strain, and Cuomo gave a frightening description of it the other day, saying that he had been blocked for eight hours by the snow. Nevertheless my first decision is wavering and I am talking again of undertaking the journey. The spirit is willing even if the flesh says it is tired. I shall see what can be done and meanwhile I have begun to think about what I should say at the opening of the congress.

January 16th

A South African poet, or rather an Englishman from South Africa of Spanish origin, Almendro by name but now calling himself by his godfather's name of Salinders, brought me a letter and a sonnet by Gawsworth, written in commemoration of the visit which he paid me three days or so ago.

January 17th

Continue thinking of the course which the Congress of Bari might pursue in case it wants or can achieve any practical action, and have decided in my mind all the details, but I must discuss it with Sforza and with other friends.

January 18th

People come to me as President of the Liberals about questions which arise in the provinces out of vanity, misery, ambition and intrigue of a kind which used to shock us, but which we have learnt by experience to tackle calmly, because without such annoyances and inconveniences life is a poor thing and liberty is lost.

January 19th

Have written my speech for the Congress, but since I have designed it myself, without being able to take advice from friends, I do not know whether revision and additions will not be necessary. I think I have said what is necessary and what can be said to the Anglo-American Allies to make them understand what Italy wants and has the right to ask, and possibly my speech, if it is circulated, may influence public opinion.

January 21st

Sforza, Omodeo and Flora have praised my speech and altogether approved it and are very satisfied with it. We looked into various probable or possible developments and renewed our intention to be rigorously intransigent, more especially as there are indications among the Socialists and Communists of a disposition to take power, while leaving things as they are, in other words collaborating with the King.[16]

[16] These detailed facts which I studied and noted most carefully and with the greatest possible exactitude provoked accusations of contradiction on my part, in view of what I say later on (under the dates of April 2nd, 4th and 6th), in a Communist review, *Rinascita,* of September 1947, p. 273. There, it is said that in my later entries I had forgotten that "for some time, for several months previous to April 1944, the Communists tended to take up this position," of "constituting a National government in order to make war." But all the parties of the Committee of Liberation tended towards this, though always with the premise that King Victor Emanuele III should be set aside, and not, as the Communists then hinted, that he should collaborate in a government like that which was set up at Brindisi. The Liberals worked efficaciously for the common goal, not only in their public speeches, articles and pamphlets, but by welcoming and developing De Nicolo's design of persuading the King to withdraw. Even the Communists, after January, appeared to have realized the expediency of this premise about the person of the King, so much so that in the first fortnight of March, after Churchill's new speech in which he wanted the King to stay, the Communists held a protest meeting together with the Socialists and the Actionists, in which the other three parties did not take part because they held such a course neither dignified nor useful and preferred the pressure or the persuasion which we ourselves might exercise upon the King. But, when Togliatli arrived and gave the word, they went back to the idea of collaborating with the King *ut sic* (followed by the Socialists but no longer by the Actionists). At this point we interfered by making public what we had already obtained in the shape of a platform for a national and democratic Government, which was far more solid than the one which they were getting ready to mount so inopportunely. And this is the truth and in telling it nothing but the truth has been set down and certainly in no spirit of competition or vanity such as has no place among the disasters of this country and among the efforts to help it, and is, thank heaven, extraneous to me.

January 23rd

Giulio Rodinò, who came with one of his sons and with Arangio Ruiz, is much perturbed by the more or less general dissatisfaction of public opinion about us, because by our intransigence we prevent the formation of a serious Government in Italy. Hence we are asked to agree to collaborate with the Prince of Piedmont if the King, as is rumoured, abdicates. Rodinò fears that one or more parties inside the Committee of Liberation may break away and enter the Royal ministerial set-up. I have little faith in an imminent abdication of the King in favour of his son; but in any case I find such a set-up absolutely repugnant and feel it to be hardly sincere and certainly dangerous. If others do not see it in this way and want to make mistakes, let them, but we must not follow them. Rodinò does not want the exclusion of the Prince to be mentioned at the Bari Congress, so that this door may be left open, and he was pleased that I had refrained from mentioning this subject in my recent speeches and political writings. I told him that in the speech I have prepared for the Bari Congress I have not mentioned the Prince either; but that in this, as in other writings to which he refers, the reason for my silence is the very opposite of the one he thinks and others believe, in that I hold the question in these respects to be definitely closed by the explicit vote of the Committee of Liberation, not to mention what I have personally written about it in the press. My friend Rodinò urged that the question should not be pressed but should be left vague at the forthcoming Bari Congress. I replied that I would certainly not reopen it, but that if others reopened it I could not prevent them, and that in case of misunderstanding I would have reiterated my already known views. When they had left, several representatives of the Liberal Party came on matters of policy concerned with the Bari Congress and we discussed the question in its various aspects. They have noted with regret that Sforza daily loses prestige because he lets himself be seen too often all over the place, talks too much and too imprudently for a future head of the Government. I replied that these things will be forgotten when we get to Rome and that Sforza, through the honesty of his life, his lively mind and his firm attitude during the whole period of Fascism and in exile, has trumps which no one else holds, even if he inevitably has defects and shortcomings. They pressed me to take the political leadership on the grounds that I had more sense of the fitness and unfitness of things and that I was more favoured because of my moderate language. I replied that such a weight would crush me, since my previous life as a scholar and not as a man of affairs or politics had not prepared me for it; moreover, that they must not forget that I am 78 and that in any case I would never outstrip Sforza who has prepared himself for the present moment by twenty years of unceasing struggle and who has the greatest confidence in me and takes counsel with me. In order not to leave him alone I have promised to accept office if need be in a Cabinet formed by him, as a Minister without portfolio, in order to take part in the Council of Ministers and to take his place as Premier if he should have to go abroad for diplomatic negotiations. As to the fear of disintegration in the Committee of Liberation, I repeated that what is important is that we, meanwhile, should not disintegrate nor put our brains into cold storage—we, who are well aware of what Italy needs at the moment.

January 25th

Parente arrived accompanied by a young man called Calvi, come from Rome after a long and adventurous roundabout journey. To my great joy Calvi brought me a note telling me of the condition of people and affairs in Rome and in central Italy. We left together for Naples and in Sforza's house there was talk with other friends. There I was given a long letter from Alfonso Casati, dated December 30th from Sardinia and addressed to Alda. What pleasure Alexander and Donna Leopolda would get from the news in this letter! I will try at least to get some of the news to them. Alfonso wants to come here and fight the Germans. Tarchiani will not come to the Congress with us. He has succeeded in getting himself landed from an English barge on the Roman coast.

January 26th

Visit from Cerabona and another representative of the Labour Democrats, a party which may have some substance elsewhere but has none here, and which we have accepted because it is said that Bonomi founded it. They kindly asked me for instructions about what is to be done at Bari. We left in two cars at 9 a.m., in one of which Sforza came with me so that we could go on talking about the situation, and with us were a few friends of the Liberal Party. We had lunch at Ariano in a little inn called *La Bolognese*. The air in the little town was icy cold and it is just as well that we did not spend the night here, as we first intended when planning the journey. When we started again Sforza went into the other car and Cianca came with us. It was a good journey. At Trani I stopped a few moments at Vecchi's printing works, to give a few instructions about work in hand. We reached Bari at 5.30 p.m. and are guests of the Laterzas, who are themselves guests in another house, since the English have requisitioned their fine villa near Bari. In the evening we saw many people and felt much keenness among those who have come, and one hopes that matters will proceed speedily and simply with few speeches and not too much oratory, and that the Congress can be guided to agreement in its conclusions. I felt much anxiety in Bari when I was told that the wireless this morning at 7 a.m. said, I know not whether rightly but certainly far too lightly, that the opposition to the Germans and the Fascists in Rome is co-ordinated by Professor Guido de Ruggiero! I remonstrated with the English officer in charge of this wireless whom I knew in Naples before the war. He declared that he had cancelled this imprudent and dangerous piece of news the night before, but he did not know how it had happened that it had been broadcast this morning.

January 27th

In the morning read several political publications and handed manuscripts and proofs in hand to Franco Laterza. Unhappily, everything in his requisitioned printing works has been at a standstill for several months because Laterza has been refused the use even of two of the thirteen machines which he asked for. Laterza's house is a sort of social centre for the Congress. I think sadly of the enthusiasm and the joy which would have filled the heart of Giovanni Laterza if he could have seen the fruits we now gather of the help which he never failed to give to our anti-Fascist opposition. At 4 p.m. went to the local Liberal Party headquarters where Sig. Laterza orders matters with zeal and intelligence. Among those who have come up from the provinces there are, of course, the ingenuous ones who, for example, propagate the idea, as though it were fresh and original, of accepting the King's invitation that we should form a government, and once having power in our hands we should send the King away. But it has been easy to silence them by explaining that their proposals are neither honest nor useful. Far more embarrassing is the other objection: what if the King does not bow to your injunction and does not withdraw, what will you do then? Will you wear the garb of moralist? Hardly respectable, politically speaking. This I was not able to counter with the story of the negotiations through De Nicola, because I have undertaken to keep them absolutely secret. When I was asked finally what should be the conclusions of the Congress, I only said that the Congress should leave behind a Commission or an executive body to carry on its work, but that as regards the composition and the powers of such a body it would be necessary to await the results of the exchange of ideas between the delegates of the six parties. I had an appointment with all these at 6 p.m., arranged by the President-Convenor of the Congress, the lawyer Cifarelli, who told me that the other delegates wanted to greet me; but as this hour went by I returned to the hall to see what had happened and there I found Professor A.P. di Meta from Sorrento, an excellent person and a kind friend, who has a weakness for 'parties,' 'organizations,' 'people in the know,' and also a weakness for extremist parties, whence naturally his membership of the Action Party. When I asked P. why on earth the delegates had not come to the appointment, he told me kindly but firmly that the three parties, Communist, Socialist and Action, had already decided among themselves what the Congress Agenda should be, that he had it in his pocket and would show it to me, but that he must state that it could not be altered even in a single comma. In my astonishment I observed that one-sided decisions like this one, made without any previous discussion with the delegates of the other parties, were not a correct procedure; but when the good man held out his hands in a grave and inexorable manner as of one who has to obey his sacred orders, I said that in that case I too knew my duty, which was to take my hat and leave. And so I did. In the evening saw Cifarelli, who is also an 'Actionist,' and told him of my qualms. I was able to read the famous resolution which is simply ridiculous,[17] and purposely

[17] A newspaper belonging to the tiny party that survived out of the Action Party has tried to quibble about my version of this incident at the Bari Congress, but in so far as it published the above-mentioned resolution—of which I took no copy—it confirms the accuracy of my version by documentary evidence. This resolution in fact proposed that the Congress should: (1) draw up an act of arraignment against the King based upon all his infringements of the Constitution; (2) that the Congress should proclaim itself the Representative Assembly of Liberated Italy and that it should be called to meet again in Rome as soon as possible, together with delegates from the still unliberated provinces, and sit there permanently until the Constituent Assembly should be formed with the following task: (a) to proceed to the formation of a Government; (b) to intensify the war effort; (c) to keep vigilant lest any one try to impinge upon the newly-acquired liberties, and meanwhile to elect a permanent executive Junta of liberated Italy, which should among other things "represent

designed to make the Congress and its delegates laugh, for it instructs the Congress Committee to step into the shoes of the King's Government immediately, administer the affairs of State and negotiate with the Allies as the true and only representative of Italy, see to supplies and put an end to the black market, etc., etc.... In other words, to exercise powers which it does not possess, and which only a Government such as we must seek to create would possess, once the King's departure had been achieved. After much discussion, in the course of which they begged me not to 'squash them with my logic' (which in truth is a power that can never squash any one, but can only redress and guide), and after an admonishment about the need for satisfying 'the masses' in their 'illusion,' about 'mundus vult decipi' (against which I once protested that such was not my profession), the whole question was put off to the morrow, when the parties will discuss the several motions before the Congress in the afternoon.

January 28th

I had hardly risen this morning when Omodeo came to see me. He had been present at yesterday's little scene and said he was grieved about the fast one which the delegates of the party to which he has given his support had tried to pull. They had, as was that party's wont, sided with the Socialists and Communists who in turn had aroused Omodeo's indignation on account of their negotiations, just begun, with Badoglio for entering the King's Ministry, and only interrupted because Badoglio would not give them the majority of the portfolios. I told him that I had already resigned myself to seeing the Congress end in no practical or useful manner, but that in any case the Congress would give me the opportunity of making a speech, boldly warning the Allies about their mistaken policy in supporting the person of the King. Shortly before 10 a.m. I went to the Piccinni Theatre where the Congress is being held and there I learned that, by order of General Alexander from Brindisi, British, American, French and Jugoslav officers may not attend the Congress; its speeches may not be broadcast and the guests in the boxes may

the Italian people in its relations with the United Nations, arrange for the lawful convocation of the Congress in the form of a representative and deliberative assembly in Rome, by examining the credentials of each delegate," etc., etc. (*Azione Meridionale,* Bari, March 30th, 1947). I think no one can deny that this resolution, drawn up by the three parties, Communist, Socialist and Actionist, without consulting the other three parties in the Committee of Liberation, is childish, and I will be forgiven if, in my irritation and impatience, instead of using this bland epithet, I used the other, as printed above.

not exceed 800 and invitations must be limited to the inaugural session only, etc. Clearly the intention is to blunt the efficacy of this solemn occasion as much as possible : it is the first of its kind in Italy since the fall of Fascism. The military and police apparatus mustered here as though a revolt were about to break out, is enormous and ridiculous. However, after the brief opening speeches by Cifarelli and Arangio Ruiz, President of the Naples Committee of Liberation, Cianca took the President's chair to direct the discussion and I was asked to speak. My speech[18] was listened to with the greatest attention and with quick understanding, to judge by the approval and applause at the salient points. At the end of it Rodinò, who served with me in Giolitti's Ministry, spoke from one of the boxes, straight from the heart, accepting and underlining the things I had said and covering me with affectionate and moving words. Sforza then proposed, almost as a corollary to my speech, that telegrams should be sent to the Governments of Great Britain, the United States, Russia, to General de Gaulle, the Jugoslavs and the Greeks. When I got home I found Sprigge and other friends; later I slept a little and then, despite the bitter and annoying cold weather, I read some history. In the evening I was told of the delegates' discussion and of the difficulty of agreeing upon the voting. The three parties of the so-called Left obstinately insist upon that resolution, so mean in its origin and stupid in its content. The Christian Democrats won't hear of an executive Junta, although they have decided to vote for the request to the King to abdicate. The Liberals, supported by the Labour Democrats, proposed giving me and Sforza a mandate to follow events and to work for the application of the Congress decisions, and we may co-opt other responsible political men who have been Ministers or held equal rank, and choose from among the party executives suitable persons for special tasks and undertakings. After a long discussion lasting till midnight, in which many delegates took part, I proposed to Cifarelli that his party should tear up its resolution, because apart from all other objections it would expose him to the jibes of all the little monarchist scribes, if for once they write intelligently. I suggested that his party should propose two distinct resolutions to be voted upon: the first for abdication, which would win an unanimous vote, and the second for the constitution of an executive Junta. For the second motion, the greatest formal courtesy towards the Christian Democrats must

[18] *La libertà italiana nella libertà del mondo* in the vol cit. *Per la nuova vita dell'Italia*, pp. 50–7.

be used, and it will be necessary to state that if they persist in their objections a Junta with a majority of five against one would be acceptable. It is likely that the Christian Democrats, who are much given to prudence or to timidity, finding themselves at this cross-roads and not wanting to be left alone and outside the majority, will end by voting with us, as they have already done on other occasions.

January 29th

Early this morning Omodeo came, and shortly afterwards Morelli and I decided to abide by the conclusions of last night's debate. I meant to go to the Congress at 3 p.m. for Sforza's concluding speech; but soon after 11 a.m. we got the news that (after an extravagant proposal to invite the black-coated workers to 'dis-obedience' had been turned down!) the delegates had reached agreement to form a Junta of six representatives, which would keep in touch with Sforza, with me and with the other elder political men who have been consistently anti-Fascist; and that the Christian Democrats had also voted for this solution. Sforza has also made his speech this morning, telling one, although this time again he did not know how to limit himself or avoid certain too highly coloured points and words. Our speeches have not been recorded for broad-casting, as had been announced, perhaps in order not to reveal the clapping at significant points, and they were read late to-night on the wireless, mine at midnight and again at 7 a.m.: a clear indica-tion of obstructionism. In the evening, visits and conversations in Laterza's house, and there I met a Cuban-Italian lady, Alba de Céspedes, author of a much read novel, *Nessuno torna indietro*. She recounted her adventures in escaping from Rome to Casoli, and then from Casoli across country occupied by the Germans, until she was able to cross the lines and reach the English. Among other adventures she spent thirty-seven days in a stable near the little vil-lage where my family come from, Montenerodomo; and she con-firmed what another refugee from the Abruzzo, from Torricella Peligna, had told me this morning, that my nephews Onorato and the other Croce brothers and sisters had only just escaped and had taken refuge at Bomba, and that during the flight one of the sisters, Elisa, died by stumbling on a mine. Alba de Céspedes told me that the village has been devastated and the old Croce house burned, as also the church of San Vito outside the walls, in the patronage of the Croce family, and its burial ground, which was built in 1757 by the priest Michele di Croce.

January 30th

We left Bari at 9 a.m., Morelli, Parente, Cassandro and Professor Lauria and I in the same car. Then at Barletta, Sforza came with us and Lauria got into another car. Lovely sunny morning. At Trani we got out for a moment to see the noble façade of the cathedral again. At Barletta we were recognized and a crowd gathered round us; and though I excused myself from getting out of the car, Sforza got out for a few minutes and greeted the people in my name also and used the occasion for a most violent tirade against a general, whose name I cannot remember, who was said to have come to this Apulian village to make propaganda for the King, and to have been one of those chiefly responsible for massacres by Italians which are said to have taken place in Jugoslavia. As we passed there were cries of hope: "Long live the saviours of Italy!" —and there was great sadness in hearing them. We stopped in Foggia to lunch in a tavern to which I used to go with friends, when in Apulia on agricultural business. In the intervals of lunch Sforza wrote the protest which I also signed, addressed to Eden, Cordell Hull and Molotov, against the attitude of the Allied authorities towards the Bari Congress. I suffered during the climb to Ariano, but once there I got out of the car, drank a coffee and felt myself normal again; big crowds round us and I saw some Neapolitan acquaintances among them. We took the road to Nocera and then to Sorrento, where we arrived shortly after 6 p.m. and I was grateful to my friends for having made this small deviation from their direct route to Naples. In the evening put the papers and documents brought from Bari in order.

Sorrento, January 31st

Revised the proofs of a new edition of my *Storia del Regno di Napoli,* and especially of the two appendices on the history of the two villages, Montenerodomo and Pescasseroli; the former (the home of my paternal family) has been destroyed as it quickly became a theatre of war in the Abruzzo, and the latter (home of my maternal family) is in danger of shortly sharing the same fate.

February 2nd

Felt very ill and tried to conquer the feeling by a walk. After an hour's sleep and a cup of coffee was able to return to my desk and write the first pages of *Proemio* (to commemorate Giovanni Laterza) for the *Critica* of 1944.

February 3rd

Finished the preface, but the day was a long one due to interruptions by the visits of groups of friends. Sforza came in the evening to tell me of: (1) his conversations with General MacFarlane and the forthcoming restitution of southern Italy to the King's Government, which in present circumstances might diminish our freedom of press and of assembly; (2) of the above General's friendly disposition towards our ideas on the abdication of the King and how we should draw his attention to the method and persons used by the King's Government. (Sforza tells me that even Ricciotti Garibaldi has appeared in Naples, the man who is said to have started and formed volunteer bands for Spain on Mussolini's behalf, and to have then denounced them to the French Government.) Sforza thinks also, what he and I never say: that the King has armed forces and the support of Churchill and of Roosevelt on his side, and that we lack any such forces. But I say: We shall see who wins, the King with his generals and admirals and occasional foreign Allies, or we with the uprightness of our demands and the logic of our actions. Sforza wants to give great prominence to the case of Ricciotti Garibaldi when talking or writing to Macfarlane, but I recommended that accurate information about his motives in coming to Naples should first be gathered, because it may be that this time the King's Government has nothing to do with it.

February 4th

At about 9 a.m. a group of cinema people appeared, who are preparing a film of the Bari Congress, and with them a good many of the delegates who live in Naples and knew that they would meet Sforza and myself here. They performed their operations on the terrace of our villa. They went away after 1 p.m. and Sforza, his son, Rodinò, Cianca and Omodeo stayed with us. After the cold up on the terrace, I had lain down to sleep in my study, when the outgoing mayor, the lawyer Cappiello, and the incoming mayor of Sorrento, the lawyer De Angelis, came to see me and I let them discourse with each other in a friendly and fervent and lengthy manner on the affairs of this commune, without my having the faintest idea what they were talking about.

February 5th

Unfortunately, hopes for an immediate entry of Rome have been dashed, and even on the Allied beach-head things seem to have come to a standstill.

February 7th

Six people from the Office of Strategic Services in Naples arrived and made me talk about immediate, indeed the only immediate and urgent problem, the cornerstone, as I called it, with some impatience. The head of the mission said he was in agreement with me; and when I was asked what the Allies could do to help us in our present situation, I replied, advise the King to abdicate. I perceive, moreover, that the fact of having passed over the Crown Prince during the Bari Congress debates has in a manner reopened the possibility of his substitution for the King. When asked about this I said that the important thing was the removal of the King, who is a direct and superannuated representative of Fascism, and that in other matters the situation can be reconsidered.

February 9th

I had begun to write some of my talks about the relation of the social classes [19] to the interpretation of history and to their political activity and life, when shortly after 9 a.m. Parente came to take me to Naples. There, in the university, I took part in a meeting about the Historical Society and its library, which was hit by a bomb in August, causing the destruction of furniture and the damaging and burial of books; and all the efforts of the librarian Parente and of the President Pontieri have not prevented the loss of several volumes through theft by soldiers and civilians, despite all possible attempts to guard the place. After Pontieri's report, we made some general provisions for restoring the library and for resuscitating the Society. Then I went to Morelli's house and from there at 3.30 p.m. to the Liberal Party headquarters, where I had promised to reply to the criticisms and demands of a group of members who are madly keen that the Liberal Party should rise to the heights of all the other

[19] Now in *Discorsi di varia filosofia*, pp. 185–94.

parties and publish a so-called 'economic programme' and should not shut itself up in 'agnosticism,' etc., etc. It is not easy, indeed it is almost impossible, to get the simple truth into the minds of people, and especially into the minds of half-educated and too talkative lawyers. Other parties make economic programmes because they are themselves essentially 'economic' parties (whether the programmes are seriously meditated or practicable is another matter). They are not 'political' or 'ethical political' parties as the Liberal Party is, which from its very foundations and in its procedure may never anticipate that which should arise concretely from free discussion and free voting. The Liberal Party neither accepts nor denies *a priori* any economic measure, and supports in practice whatever in practice and in a given situation will promote and not suppress freedom and a civilized and moral life. I succeeded in explaining this concept in my reply to these members whom I found gathered at the Party headquarters; but although I left them short of arguments, I do not flatter myself that I persuaded them, nor do I think that this would be psychologically possible. As for those who were pining for economic programmes, I advised and exhorted them to study the various problems or, at least, a certain number of them which go by the name of economic, and so to outline possible solutions by their own study and after discussion with friends and with fellow Party members, solutions which must necessarily retain the character of abstract and casuistical exercises, pending an election, a Parliament and voting. Went to Sforza's house, where General Macfarlane was invited to lunch. Spoke with him about the question of the King, and we both clearly told him our ideas on the subject. Macfarlane had come from Salerno where he had spoken with Badoglio, whom he had much liked. Unfortunately, I learnt from him, with great grief, of the death of Major Malcolm Munthe and a comrade of his near Anzio, as a result of having been hit by a bomb. Macfarlane had had him on his staff in Gibraltar and thought much of him; I and my friends have had innumerable proofs of kindness and friendliness from him. It was he who last September went from Capri to Sorrento with Brindisi and fetched Adelina and Alda; and I saw him several times again afterwards. (To my great joy I learned later that he had only been seriously wounded and I got a greeting from him before he went to England to convalesce.) In the evening an American officer came to see me in Sforza's house and brought me a letter from Chicago from the Editor of *Living Philosophers*, to which I am asked to reply and thereby re-establish philosophical relations. In these times! (I am not philosophical to that degree nor in that way.) I took the long letter with me to read and ponder at leisure in Sorrento; I see that the letter insists that I should send an epilogue dealing with the criticisms of my work according to the plan of that publication. But I have already sent a brief epilogue and I do not intend to pursue the matter, because I choose those critics to whom I believe it is worthwhile to reply, and I do not reply to any old eavesdropper or beginner. If they do not want to publish this big tome about me, which I have never asked for, so be it.[20] The officer told me that a Chair has been endowed at Chicago for the teaching of my philosophy!

February 10th

In the morning, in Sforza's house, many visits on various matters about which I was asked for help or advice, but mostly these were troubled minds letting off steam, such as one hears in almost every conversation just now, and which trouble our hearts, already troubled enough. Parente accompanied me back to Sorrento; fine sunshine revived our low spirits, but after midday the bad weather, which has fraternally accompanied a private sadness, began again. A Scottish captain and a friend of his came to ask me for explanations about Italian matters, about which they know practically nothing, and I do not know whether they care. This is a *corvée* to which I have to submit, and it is all the heavier in that I doubt its utility. Looked over the many papers and proofs which have been accumulating, and began to get through some of them. Turned over the pages of a batch of documents and of political news given me by Raimondo. But here, a catastrophe! Having been called to supper, just as I was going as usual to wash my hands in the wash-place off the hall, I tripped over a zinc box, put there without my knowledge, across the entrance, where it had never been, so that I fell heavily on the other side, protecting my head from the wall with my left arm. But I could not get up again because my arm was now useless, so I sat down on the ground and waited for the maid to come and call me again, which happened, and then I asked them to tell Raimondo, who came to help me up, and I went down to dinner with him. The doctor was called and diagnosed a lesion or a sprain. Let us hope that it is nothing more; but I spent a bad night.

[20] With exquisite kindness, the undertaker of this publication has informed me that, since my decision is unshakeable, he will publish the collection "when I am dead." A bibliographical titbit for my readers.

February 11th

Visit this morning to my bedside of Senator De Lorenzo, whom I have not seen for some years, asking me officially on behalf of all the members of the four Royal Academies of Naples and on behalf of the Allied authorities to assume the Presidency of these, pending their reconstitution. But I excused myself because I have neither the time nor the desire to busy myself with academies, and the Neapolitan ones have lost their most important asset, the library, burnt by the Germans in September. They also burnt the library of the Pontaniana Academy and its fine collection, and some codices and a miscellaneous manuscript in several volumes about the old Ponaninana at the time of the Renaissance (given to the Duchess of Andria who gave it to me and I gave it to the Academy). Would I had kept them in my library! I also refused to rejoin the Academy of Moral and Political Sciences, from which I had been expelled for having refused to take the oath of loyalty to the regime. Why go back among them when no happy memory binds me to them and when I will not have, as I formerly had, any works to offer to the Academy? We shall have to await an epuration of their members for political misdemeanours which is an operation in which I, on no account, need be concerned. (Among the Italian academies the only one in which I intend to stay is the Venetian Institute, which did not ask me for any oath, did not cancel my name from the list of members and sent the proof of its yearly report for me to add my titles to my name, so that I, imagining some mistake on the part of the secretary, put down a series of 'ex-' and an etc. to the titles of which Fascism had deprived me, and with as many more 'etc.' I added those of the foreign academies and universities to which I belong; a jolly list, which to my amazement I saw printed *ad literam* in the annual report, and repeated every year, when they sent me the proofs in case there should be anything to add or modify, which there was not, and laughing to myself, I used to put 'all right' on my proof. Their frankness and courage naturally found me grateful and faithful.) The surgeon came and with much ability and quickness, though causing me acute pain, took advantage of a moment when I was about to faint to reset my dislocated bone. It remains to be seen whether there will be anything else wrong with my arm; for that purpose an X-ray will be necessary.

February 13th

Raimondo brought a radiologist from Naples and the X-ray shows, apart from a dent, a fracture in the collar bone. But Dr. Morelli, having only just learned of the incident, affectionately came over from Naples and advised another X-ray in a Naples hospital.

Naples, February 14th

Only slept for a few hours last night, and when I got up I started work again on an interrupted article. Dr. Morelli with Parente came to take me to the Villa dei Gerani at Capodimonte, where the surgeon, Professor Del Torto, took another X-ray which showed that my arm was fractured in a place different from the one on the photograph taken in Sorrento. I do not speak of the operation which ensued, during which I did not shout, because it would have been useless. In the room which has been allotted to me I saw Omodeo and other friends, who talked of political and university matters.

February 15th

Sforza and Tarchiani came to see me to discuss the political attitude of the British and particularly of General Macfarlane, and other political matters of the moment.

February 16th

Made a few notes, but the necessary concentration for straight writing is not possible because of many visitors. Among other visitors the departing British Commissioner for Education, Grayen, and his successor Smith, who brought me a letter from London from Mrs. Sprigge with several papers and pamphlets, which contained notable pages.

February 17th

Apart from Morelli and the others, a most affectionate visit from Signora Bakunin Caccioppoli. Later Del Secolo came asking my advice about a new proposal from the Allied press office to entrust him with the only newspaper being printed in Naples. He is asked to remain neutral about the question of the King and to print news from the conflicting parties on both sides. A little temperature on and off, so that the doctor has decided to postpone my return to Sorrento, which had been fixed for to-morrow.

February 18th

An unexpected and welcome visit from my friend Dr. Rosati, whom I had not seen for months because he had remained in his village of Abruzzo on account of the German invasion. He could only come to Naples for a few days in the company of a British officer. His experience in the Abruzzo of the attitude of the British towards the Italians convinced him that they simply intend to keep Italy under, to prevent Italy from recovering, from fighting and from rising again, and that this is why they favour the Government of the King and of Badoglio, which is a weak Government, offering no obstacles or complications. This dark anxiety unfortunately pervades my mind, and the mind of every Italian who cares about the future of his country.

February 21st

In the evening Renato Morelli told me that De Nicola has finally seen the King and had had a long conversation and discussion with him on the 19th and 20th and that the King in the end resolved to withdraw, leaving his son as Lieutenant-General of the Realm. De Nicola is to come to-morrow to tell me about it in detail.

February 22nd

A long night, and slept on and off from 9 p.m. to 7 a.m. Thought over the situation which is moving in new directions with new perils, and thought of new difficulties to be faced, all of which was accompanied by a painful awareness of my temporary disability and by the fear of a permanent weakening of my bodily strength—or indeed of my mental capacity in matters of will and action. In the early afternoon De Nicola came with Morelli and told me, in greater detail and with more clarity, of his conversation with the King at Ravello and of the immediate consequences. Contrary to rumours, which may have been purposely spread, he found the King far from willing to abdicate or to go away. De Nicola urgently demonstrated to the King how the road which he had decided to take and would not abandon could only lead to his own and the monarchy's downfall. The King said he had the armed forces with him, but they could only achieve a reactionary and oppressive and necessarily ephemeral Government ending in violent opposition. The King recognized that such was the situation and that the deductions and previsions arising out of it were justified; he asked De Nicola his opinion about an alternative solution. De Nicola answered frankly: withdraw and leave a Lieutenant-Generalcy up to such time as the Italian people can decide upon the form of the State they want. The King did not contest this right of the people and the need that they should exercise it. But the King's resistance grew again when dealing with the matter of the Lieutenant-Generalcy, which should be entrusted to his son, and De Nicola proved to him that all the objections and difficulties which he raised were not directed against the Lieutenant-Generalcy, but against the decision to go away himself, although he had recognized the necessity for this step. All this lasted four hours and at the end of it the King said he would think it over again. As the evening was already coming on, the King observed that it would be too inconvenient for De Nicola to return to Torre del Greco, and invited him to dine and to spend the night at Ravello, and called Duke Acquarone to make the necessary dispositions. When Acquarone appeared, the King informed him of the discussions with and the views of De Nicola, and described the stage which the question had reached; he asked him what he thought about it. Acquarone replied that the terms within which De Nicola had circumscribed the situation were most accurate and that the dilemma would have to be resolved: either reaction with an obscure and desperate future, or the King must go away and the Lieutenant-Generalcy be established. After a break and an exchange of looks with Acquarone, the latter asked De Nicola whether, if the King should not accept the idea of the Lieutenant-Generalcy, De Nicola could still be counted upon? De Nicola replied: absolutely no, adding that he would then make his intention public as well as the steps he had taken. Thereupon the King declared that he would forthwith accept the Lieutenant-Generalcy. Nevertheless, De Nicola prudently insisted that he should not thus immediately give his final assent but should think it over again. De Nicola would leave at dawn and the King could send his final reply through Acquarone to Torre del Greco. The Prince of Piedmont, who had come to spend the Sunday with his mother, then arrived, and the whole thing was fairly melancholy, in a dimly lit room, with the Queen who had nothing to say and the Prince who said nothing, unless it were to answer questions put to him by his father, and the King who spoke of several places he had visited in Calabria and of other matters extraneous to his visitors. The next day, Sunday, at Torre del Greco, in the afternoon, De Nicola received the visit of Acquarone, who confirmed the King's acceptance and with whom he exchanged ideas about the execution of the matter, because, if the proclamation announcing the Lieutenant-Generalcy is to be published immediately (and De Nicola has been entrusted with the drafting of it) the transfer of powers to the Lieutenant-General should occur after the liberation of Rome, and the delay would be necessary for practical reasons of residence, and suchlike. De Nicola in turn suggested that the Allied authorities and Badoglio should be quickly informed of what had been decided. The King in his conversation with De Nicola had maintained a reserved and correct attitude when mentioning Sforza; but was profuse in praise of my loyalty and patriotism, which he said was the sole motive of my attitude; and he began to ask anxiously for news about my accident. De Nicola observed that I am perhaps the only true monarchist in Italy who is still devoted to a constitutional monarchy and the King agreed to this judgment. Such are the labours accomplished by De Nicola with wisdom and with perspicacity, and it is the only practical action which has so far been accomplished, I say the only achievement, in the field of political events. De Nicola has some doubts about the warmth with which Sforza will accept these results and fears the influence upon him of those who surround him. But I reassured him on this point and begged him to inform Sforza directly and personally of what he had done and then to come back to me with Sforza, for unfortunately I cannot move out of this nursing home. However, in the afternoon Sforza came to visit me, unaware of the conversations which have taken place, and I myself informed him and received from him new proof of the importance of De Nicola's step and found Sforza quite ready to enter into the scheme and to collaborate. Later Renato Morelli told me that De Nicola and Sforza will meet in his house and that after to-morrow the former will come to see me.

February 23rd

Woke up ill at ease and the depression continued during the morning; this afternoon I feel considerably relieved, perhaps because a slight temperature, which I have had all these days, has finally gone down. Continuous visits and continuous listening to the usual cheerful conversations which do not alter matters an inch; they stand still or pursue their own course. In the evening with Morelli, Parente and other friends talked again of the pressure, indeed of the obstinate demands, which some members of the Liberal Party are making for an additional 'economic programme.' As I said, I give up trying to reinforce certain brains which are better left to splutter and evaporate and I prefer simply to reply jokingly. But I have proposed that these claimants should be invited to write a programme for themselves and we shall see what comes out of it, for either it will be super-generic and insipid or it will be arbitrary and quack, worthy perhaps of other parties but not of ours, which is serious in its concepts. But I am troubled to-day by Churchill's speech which supports the King's government or, as he likes to say, Marshall Badoglio's, and repudiates or postpones our requests. This, however, will certainly not cause us to change our course, but it might induce the King not to fulfil his commitments to De Nicola.

February 24th

At noon De Nicola and Sforza, and with them Morelli and I re-examined the situation after Churchill's speech. De Nicola is quite certain that the King will abide by his commitments, and he refuses even to consider a contrary development. Moreover he has an appointment to-day with General Macfarlane, with whom it seems Sforza is also to have a meeting. He has written a reply to Churchill to prove to him that he has been badly informed in the matters he has dealt with, and I also signed this, after he had somewhat tempered it, and Sforza resolved to give it to Macfarlane to pass on through the right channels.

February 25th

Am 78 to-day. About 2 p.m. De Nicola came with Morelli to tell me of his visit to General Macfarlane, who had an American officer with him and later called in some 'experts.' They listened with great attention to the results of the conversation between De Nicola and the King, and by dint of questioning succeeded in understanding the situation clearly. Among other things they asked whether the new Ministry which is to take the place of the royal one can possibly be more vigorous than the present one? To which De Nicola replied that the present royal Ministry has no political strength behind it, whereas the new one would be backed by the Committees of Liberation composed of the parties. To the question whether these would reach agreement to support it, he replied that three at least, the Liberal Party, the Christian Democrats and the Labour Democrats, in other words those which the Allies call the Centre, would immediately back it, recognizing Croce's authority; and that as for the other three, although he could not speak of them with the same certainty, he thought they would, especially as two of them, the socialistic and the communistic ones, had previously been disposed to collaborate with Badoglio's government, the former if it had obtained a majority of the Ministries and the latter if the King would abdicate. After that they asked him another and a delicate question: whom did he envisage as Prime Minister? De Nicola replied: either Croce or Sforza, but the former will not hear of it, and the latter meets with obstacles, although Croce himself, who would have a greater following in public opinion on account of his moderation, resolutely supports Sforza. They then cleared up other details about the time and the procedure. De Nicola's impression is that they attached great importance to the King's agreement to retire and to the investiture of the Lieutenant-Generalcy; but naturally they did not otherwise express themselves. During the second half of the day I had a painful conversation with political men here, who insist that I should accept the Premiership in the next democratic Ministry, instead of Sforza, who has done himself a good deal of harm, according to a general impression, by the aggressive tone and the too virulent words and too strong images he uses in his speeches; and I had to declare firmly that I did not feel I had the necessary experience or endowments with which to govern my country, and that my refusal was not due only to a repugnance to pass over Sforza, my old colleague in Giolitti's Ministry, with whom I have had the closest relations during more than twenty years of vicissitudes and exile and who has the greatest confidence in me and hears my advice with much deference and gentleness, but was due above all to a knowledge of the limitations, as I said, of my ability and my strength. I said that if I had felt like Achilles, in fact if I had believed myself possessed of the required ability, I would frankly and honestly have said so to Sforza, and have put myself forward as his colleague or even as his competitor, and would not constantly have backed his candidature as I have done. Finally Sforza came, and I told him of De Nicola's conversation with Macfarlane and the other Allied representatives, but not of course of the rest. Then, when he made me read another and most vivacious interview with a great American newspaper in which he inveighs against the nomination by the King's government of Zaniboni (the man who made an attempt on Mussolini's life) to the post of Supreme Magistrate for the political epuration of those guilty of or tainted with Fascism, I took the opportunity of recommending once more that he should put a brake upon his polemical explosions. I told him that he was miraculously turning me, a born polemicist who had spent all my life using the most varied argumentative instruments from high emotion to jokes and leg-pulls, into someone with a reputation for a quiet, moderate and mild temperament, by dint of comparing what I say with what he says. He confessed, for his part, that he does not succeed in correcting the exuberance of his temperament because he fears that by so doing he would lose its quality, that is its impetus.

Sorrento, February 26th

Returned to Sorrento this morning, accompanied by Dr. Morelli and Parente.

February 27th

Went through correspondence of the last few days and put aside the few letters to which I shall have to reply: most of them are requests for personal services, most varied ones and even extravagant ones, like the one from a mother-in-law who asks my intervention in order to re-establish harmonious relations with her daughter-in-law, from whom she is separated. (This reminded me that in ancient popular Neapolitan music one of the most noisy and strident instruments was amusingly called 'socra e nocra'!) It is incredible how so many prosaic and often most complicated services can be solicited from a man of my age who is already, under present conditions, tormented by the thought of not being able to do what is necessary in the many duties of a public nature in which he is involved. And it is a proof of the irresponsible egotism of people who had cancelled me from the living these twenty years and never asked me for anything, that they should now, upon hearing my name re-echoing, attribute fantastic power and healing virtue to it, and cling to me, trying to pull me each his own way, without any respect and, I would say, without any pity. The lawyer Papa came to tell me that the Allied authorities have decided to hand over the only permitted daily in Naples to Del Secolo, who inspires them with most confidence on account of his seriousness and honesty: this is a solution which I, when asked, had proposed to the Allied press office (or 'psychological propaganda' office) ever since the early days of last October but which was stupidly torpedoed by the Committee of Liberation (I was then in Capri). They understood nothing about it and, without weighing my proposal, they voted against it. Now—after five months, after the evil experiences they have had and by reason of the logic in things—my proposal has been adopted. Better late than never.

February 28th

The Allied governor Musmanno, just back from Cassino, tells me of the disappearance down there of entire towns and villages and of the destruction of the historical abbey: the news was a very sad blow. All the losses which have already occurred, all those yet to come, the monuments, the documents of Italian history which may be destroyed, find no adequate comfort in the thought that these losses and ruins do not deprive man of the creative force of the spirit, which will rebuild, as in the past, a new world over the old. The things that are now being lost are not merely material things but instruments of the spiritual life and I feel for them a kind of pain and anxiety like that of the miser for his accumulated riches.

February 29th

Have written articles which may serve for the new Liberal weekly in Naples. Unexpectedly the Polish Count G., a former diplomat, arrived, whom I had not seen since 1942. After the armistice had been published he left Rome with one of his sons, and after twenty days' journey on foot, reached Termoli and joined the British army, in which he has been serving all these months in various offices and missions. He has sent his son to England to study in a Benedictine college. He has no news of his wife or of his other sons and daughters, who have stayed behind in German-occupied cities. He is most cheerful, happy and grown younger, although he must be over fifty: he says he has never enjoyed life more. This does not prevent his outlook from being far from optimistic, for he is persuaded that the real war will be waged later on between Anglo-Saxon and Russian imperialism, and that the United States and Britain have no interest in definitive action so long as Russia and Germany smash at each other reciprocally. He only believes 'fifty per cent,' as he says, in the much advertised great Western offensive in the spring. On the other hand, he too thinks that Germany is far from being defeated or dismayed. Germany has given up the badly-planned and unsuccessful conquest of Russia, but is retiring in good order and strengthening itself inside its central European fortress; German prisoners are full of boastful confidence and say that Germany is prepared for another five years of war and is waiting to see what happens. He foresees as not unlikely a very rapid Bolshevization of Europe, particularly of Germany and of France. In the latter the fire of eighteenth century patriotism, still felt in the 1914 war, no longer burns. The French now fighting in Italy are Moroccan troops; the French proper, with a few rare exceptions, no longer have the spirit or the will to fight, etc. This is the outlook and the forecast of a politician. After which shall I envy the happy disposition which allows men like G. to enjoy life, despite the ruin, nay the disappearance of their country and notwithstanding the imminent ruin of European civilization? I asked of him: "When all is said and done have German or Russian imperialism any new word to say to the heart of man?" He answered: "Anglo-American imperialism has no new word either to say." And I: "But this word is liberty, it is civilization which is always new because it eternally triumphs." And he concluded (but pretty coldly, with his usual tone of indifference): "Just because of that we must hope that the Anglo-Saxon will prevail."

March 1st

Thinking it over, there is something to be gained from G's disposition yesterday, which so amazed me. It is this: that we, in the fastnesses of our hearts, still expect a world to arise like the one— a continuation of the one—in which we were living for several decades before the war of 1914, a world of peace, work, national and international collaboration. Here is the spring of our unmitigated anxiety, because these hopes grow ever dimmer and, worse still, become troubled and obscure. We must not expect the rebirth of that world, its revival and improvement, but we must expect an interminable sequence of clashes, and upsets and ruin due to revolutions and wars, which will cover a half century or more, and may even achieve nothing positive, but only lead to the *finis Europæ*. We must resolutely detach ourselves from such hopes, and get accustomed to the idea of living a life without stability, upon which we can no longer weave the old individual and socially ordered activities; it will be a day-to-day life, so repugnant to us who were men who laboured, who set ourselves well thought-out programmes and carried them calmly through. Upon this scene, faltering at every step, we must do the best we can to live with dignity, as men, thinking, working, nursing the gentle affections, and be ever ready to give up, without on that account becoming low-spirited. The proposition is much easier to formulate than to carry out; but since we have no other at our disposal, we must ever remember it and graft it within us, so as to modify to some extent the old Adam. We shall certainly never reach the point of clasping to our hearts the *aes triplex* of indifference. A sense of disorientation there will always remain, or it will be renewed—a lack of support, an instability, a discontent, a being ill-at-ease; and this, in the end, will make us welcome death more amicably.

March 2nd

I see Captain Sylvester here (Salvadori) where he has come to convalesce. He is a dear and good boy, intelligent and lively.

March 3rd

Renato Morelli tells me that Sforza is rather depressed; but I do not see what else we could have done, given that collaboration with the King was impossible with diffidence on both sides, and that in any case such collaboration would have prevented and corrupted the hoped-for regeneration of Italian life. Even if such a corruption should unfortunately occur, we must not be its promoters. On the other hand, De Nicola's action had granted us the full victory once the King had assented to our request to surrender his powers (an undertaking upon which he has not gone back, nor otherwise questioned, up till to-day); and the obstacle to our policy comes from Churchill's speech, which itself is born of the unhappy course of the war in Italy and generally in Europe, of the strength of Germany's resistance and of the need to control the English Conservatives who still make love to Fascism, just as they did to Nazism and to Franco. So we shall have to see how we can remove the new obstacle which has arisen.

March 4th

I carry on my present literary work with alacrity, yet my thoughts continually return to the present situation of the war, of politics and especially of Italy in all this. My conclusions about Italy are: given the proposition of English politicians, represented by Churchill, to uphold the King and the Fascistical elements in Italy whom they deem to be conservative, all we can do is to try to get English political men to come to Italy as authoritative and impartial observers, so that they see how things really are and make them known to England and work on public opinion which opposes conservative currents. Friend Sforza has counted too much on his conversations with Macfarlane and with other British people who are here, who are correct and kind in listening and in talking, but are conservatives too, and in any case, are subservient to Churchill's policy, and as military men could not pursue, and could certainly not conceive of, any other.

March 5th

Visit from the new American Civil Affairs Officer, Colonel Poletti, with whom I spokc concerning current questions and who seemed to me clearly intentioned in a Liberal way, or as he says in a democratic way, and fairly experienced through having had to deal with and settle similar affairs in Sicily.

March 6th

I sketched out replies to a few political questions which Sprigge has put to me and I have asked Max Salvadori to ask him what he intends doing with them, and whether the newspapers will use them seriously, in which case I will give them to him. If not, I will not do so, because I am tired of always repeating the same thing for the benefit of journalists who have to have something to put in their correspondence. I have refused to see several of them recently, giving as a reason the state of my health.

Naples, March 9th

Dr. Morelli and Parente came, and with them and Alda, who nurses me, I went back to the nursing home in Naples. Here the X-ray showed that the fracture has mended perfectly. Sforza came to inform me of the little that is new in the political situation.

March 11th

Corbino, who is at present one of the Ministers of the King, came and described the not too happy condition in which they find themselves on account of the King's remaining, and on account of the relations with the Allies who penetrate everywhere and are incompetent. In the provinces which have been restored to the Royal government things are disordered and confused; unsuitable men have been put into office, no account has been taken of seniority and large increases of pay have caused great waste; nor can any of all this be modified without the consent of the Allied authorities. Corbino does not think that things can go on in this way and believes that resignation must take place, if not of the whole Ministry (for some are attached to their offices), at least of a group of Ministers among whom he mentioned, apart from himself, the Minister of Justice, who is the Magistrate Casati, De Caro and perhaps Cuomo. I said that they should take this step, not only in order to accelerate a solution, but also that they who are technically able may not find themselves outside public life, now that there is a great scarcity of capable men in Italy.

March 12th

Renato Morelli told me of the regulations for epuration decided upon yesterday by the Committee of Liberation in Naples; among them is one for senators nominated after January 3rd, 1925, which is so anti-juridical that I have written at once to Poletti about it and he will have to examine it.

March 14th

Slept little and badly on account of pain in my arm, now out of plaster. The very gentle massage which the nun on duty gave me calmed and dispelled the pain. In the morning, in order to shake myself and revive myself, I wrote a little article for the Liberal weekly on the translation of one of Stalin's pamphlets which has been printed here in Naples (I am told, in 120,000 copies) and pretty widely circulated by the Communists. My article was half serious, half comic, and bade the Communists here in Naples work on a level with the culture of Italy, which is much higher than that of Russian readers.[21] The Allies have finally entrusted Del Secolo with the editorship of the only Naples daily, in accordance with my old proposal. Actually I made the proposal thinking that they wanted to publish a Liberal newspaper, but now they have made the con-

[21] This is now in *Per la nuova vita dell'Italia*, pp. 66–70.

dition that it be neutral in Party questions, and also in those concerning the King, which has perplexed Del Secolo, who made a reservation that he would ask my advice about that. But I advised him to accept the newspaper, even in its watered-down and constricted form, and to get all the good he can out of it, and gradually slacken the restrictions.

March 15th

Heavy German air raid to-night met by brilliant and noisy anti-aircraft defences. Twenty minutes after I had gone to bed in this deafening noise, and unable to move because of a metal frame, Professor Del Torto came to ask me whether Alda and I would like to go down to the shelter, where all the other patients already were. Much surprised I asked him how that would be possible and he replied: "With the whole bed inside the lift." In fact, the nuns put some little wheels on to the bed and in a few minutes got me down into the underground shelter! In the morning confabulations with Morelli and Parente about the weekly *La libertà*. Later De Nicola came and brought such grave news about the casualties and the ruins of this night, and such painful news of the destruction of the Church of Monteoliveto (first Santa Chiara, the museum of the Angevin Kings, now Monteoliveto, the museum of the Kings of the House of Aragon!) that my mind was paralysed and I could not discuss political matters with De Nicola as I should have done, for they were the object of our conversation. Briefly, the situation now seems to be like this. The King insists on having the formula of the proclamation by which he will announce his determination to retire and to make his son Lieutenant-General. De Nicola was of the opinion that this act should be deferred for a few weeks because, after the demonstration held last Sunday in Naples, the King's determination and the Proclamation might be misunderstood as a victory of the three extremist Parties (the Communist, Socialist and—who knows why?—the Actionists), who organized and carried out this demonstration without consulting the other three Parties. Those who saw it, both Italian and foreigners, say that it ended not in a protest against Churchill's speech, but in a Communist assertion which threw the other two Parties, especially the Action Party, into the shade. At the most, Badoglio might be tempted to form a new royal Ministry with the Communists and with socialistic and communistic elements, an idea which was adumbrated last January.

There is reason to believe that the Allies, informed of the King's intention and undertaking, have decided to reconsider the question, all of which links up with Sprigge's questions, especially the question of my reserve about deferring the practical application of the Lieutenant-Generalcy until after the liberation of Rome. Spoke with De Nicola also about another of his intentions, which is to enlarge our reconstituted Liberal Party into a Liberal Union, about which we agreed to talk further in a later meeting. Later Sforza came with the usual friends and then Del Secolo, with whom I exchanged ideas about the newspaper he is about to edit, and I indicated certain problems of civic interest which need illumination.

March 16th

Tormented by the usual pains last night and awake for several hours. Sequence of visitors: among them a young priest who came to bring me words of praise from the Venerable Maria Landi (the 'holy nun' of whom so much has been spoken in recent years in Naples and who is said to be intimately associated with the Duchess of Aosta and with other authorities, and to be a great manipulatrix of affairs and of intrigues), and several pictures of a Madonna who should be venerated, she says, and in whose honour she has already begun to build a temple. Also Senator D'Amato, the most famous doctor in Naples; Maiuri, Director of the Museum, who expressed gratitude for my spontaneous defence of those who were threatened with 'epuration' merely because they had been nominated as members of the Italian Academy; Giulio Rodinò, with whom I had a close talk for two hours and who said clever and wise things about present conditions in Italy, and with the kind of feeling I share; and finally, the Archbishop of Naples, Cardinal Ascalesi, who, having come to visit this nursing home, courteously visited me also in my room, to wish me a speedy recovery. Rodinò is also tormented by doubts about the solidity of a Ministry, if we can form one, to take the place of the King's very weak Cabinet. He is certain that De Nicola, who is so clever in analysing a situation and so able in negotiation, will not in any event wish to join such a Ministry, by reason of his temperament, as demonstrated on other occasions. Rodinò is sceptical about Sforza's tact and prudence, and agrees with the criticisms that have been made about his speeches. Rodinò was persuaded by the detailed reasons for my unwillingness to take Sforza's place at any cost, but he was none the less doubtful about the lack, here in Naples, of a suitable Prime Minister or of proven men to assist, temper and support a Premier. For my part I reminded him of Sforza's good qualities and I ended by saying that he must be tried out.

March 17th

To-night more horrible pain in my arm and beneficial assistance by the nun, who with long and patient massage and a harmless soporific procured for me a few hours sleep. Nevertheless, in a wakeful interval, I pondered over De Nicola's idea of changing the Liberal Party into a Liberal Union, which at first seemed a good one to me, but of which I now see the weakness and the inconveniences. Another visit from Poletti who asked my advice on several matters and about several people, which I gave him. The line which I took last January in my letter to the Liberal Party about the rules which shall govern epuration has been adopted, with the support of Poletti himself.

March 18th

Long conversation with De Nicola in the presence of Morelli. De Nicola thinks, on the question of turning the Liberal Party into a Liberal Union, that an appeal should be made by public invitation to Liberals or more-or-less Liberals, who can find no parties to join. This seems to me of little use, and not without possibilities of equivocation. If anything, I would sooner appeal (which procedure he excludes) to those parties which are not intrinsically and by their institutions anti-Liberal, as the Communists and Catholics or Christian Democrats are. Such an appeal should prove that whenever other parties accept and profess the Liberal method, they are Liberal and their economic programme need be no obstacle, and that indeed the Liberal Party does not forbid but welcomes such programmes, provided they be discussed and submitted to the vote of the majority. The Liberal Party does not draw up its own economic programme because its tasks are primarily ethico-political and this is the premise of all its economic debates and decisions, open to the adherence of members as single persons or as groups. But the fundamental doctrine does not admit individual exceptions or divisions into groups. We also separately re-examined the difficulties inherent in the constitution of a Ministry; but when I insisted that De Nicola should belong to it together with Rodinò, serving under Sforza, and said that in this case I would be ready to co-operate in some form or other. I met with a not unexpected but extremely solid resolution to take no part in the Government. Although he said, as he was leaving, that he would continue this conversation during a further visit to me at Sorrento, I believe that this was only a formal courtesy and that there is no hope of winning him over. Del Secolo made me read his preface to the first number of *Risorgimento* of which he has become the editor. Two Communists came to see me, Eugenio Reale and the editor of the Communist weekly in Naples, Valenzi; then Cerabona and others belonging to the Labour Democrats; then Angelico Venuti, a Catholic and editor of the Christian Democrat weekly, a dear and good person; and then Selvaggi, who is the likely prefect for the province of Naples; and, in the evening, Sforza.

Sorrento, March 19th

Returned to Sorrento. After breakfast talked at length with Morelli and other friends, explaining my ideas about the widening of the Liberal Party.

March 20th

Raimondo, who has come back from Bari, outlined what the Italian Committee formed by the American authorities for guerilla warfare in northern Italy, has already done, and is proposing to do. He tells me that he has news of the keenness and the actions of the partisans, and that it has been fairly damaging for the Germans.

March 21st to April 1st

I make no separate notes for these days because my convalescence, just begun, gives me greater pain and is more of a nuisance than was the accident. The twenty-first was my name day and I defended myself as best I could from visitors bringing wishes; however, I came down from my study to the dining-room because I realized that Adelina did not want to see my place empty at the table. A visit from Piccardi at 11 p.m. He was once in Badoglio's Ministry and is now an officer in the Italian section of the front, and among other things he said that the young Italian soldiers now do their duty without political fervour of any kind, but as people who have become used to war over a number of years, so that from this point of view things are better. Like me he thinks that the moment of enthusiasm in which shoals of volunteers could and should have been enlisted, when so many wanted to be and wanted to fight and were disillusioned at not finding a welcome or orders, is now over, because of the attitude taken and the negotiations carried out by the royal government, which is diffident of the Republican spirit of most of those volunteers. A visit from Minifie on the 24th, from the Anglo-American propaganda offices, and from Greenless, transferred from Naples to Bari, whom I knew and often saw before the declaration of war against Britain, for he was one of the heads of the British Institute, whose premises were on an upper floor of the house I live in at Naples. The gentleman who was head of Italy then, either as a pretence or as a joke, allowed the Institute to be solemnly inaugurated in the presence of the British Ambassador at the end of 1939, while himself working to draw Italy into war against England. R. G. Bolton, an English student of modern languages and literature came to see me on the 25th. Thank heaven he was indifferent to politics and did not plague me with the usual questions, but talked for a couple of hours of Bibliophily, which he cultivates, and he showed me several books and manuscripts purchased in Naples, which I was able to enlarge upon and judge. A Polish soldier also came, Gustav Herling Grundzinski, a student of philosophy, a reader of my books in German translation, and a member of a group in Warsaw who study my philosophy. He wants to translate my books into Polish. In the evening a visit from the lawyer Cafiero, who runs the Neapolitan journalists' organization, whom I urged to approve the collaboration of Del Secolo and the other staff writers on the *Risorgimento* with our weekly *La Libertà,* although such a procedure is usually forbidden in journalistic contracts. But allowances might be justified now, because no political party ideas or tendencies, not even Liberal ones, may now be expounded in the *Risorgimento.* At dawn a rain of ashes, due to the eruption of the Vesuvius, darkened the sky and a bad day began. Immediate steps had to be taken to remove the weight of the ashes from the terraces of the villa and to take away the ashes which have got into the house and covered the windows of the balconies. Flora came on the 26th and to my great comfort brought me better news than I previously had about the damage to the Church of Monteoliveto, during the last German air raid on Naples. Some chapels have indeed been pierced, and Rossellino's sculptures, those of Giovanni Nola, of Santacroce and others have tumbled, but the sculptures have only been slightly damaged because they were protectively wrapped and this proved efficacious. In the evening I received a long political letter from Omodeo, an impassioned letter, troubled in its facts and in its judgments, to which I replied at length, clearly and in detail, in such a way as to reassure him of my unchanging affection and solid ties. Renato Morelli, Parente and Cassandro came on the 27th to ask whether it was now advisable to publish the King's undertaking to De Nicola? I replied that any further delay was dangerous and might prove harmful. There were inacceptable things in the undertaking (such as the postponement of the institution of the Lieutenant-Generalcy until after the liberation of Rome), but since this demand by the King is a spontaneous and unilateral act which we do not have to reciprocate, we can always take up this question again. A visit from Colonel Hume, about to become a General, and now transferred to Caserta, and a visit from the Chief of Staff of General Clark, who, when he referred to the war round Cassino, kept saying every moment, 'difficult!' Del Secolo, Venuti, the editor of the Catholic Weekly, Omodeo, Sforza, his son and other friends all came on the 28th; Sforza stayed with us and I asked him to go to see De Nicola in Naples to-morrow and tell him that I think that the publication of the King's proclamation should not be delayed, especially as the news of it has leaked out and is being discussed. Weariness and sickness on the 29th and 30th, of which I took advantage to do much literary work, and also worked out a speech on the political parties in Italy and on the aims and methods of the revived Liberal Party. On the 31st took counsel with Morelli, Parente and Cassandro, on certain lines of newspaper polemics to be followed in the columns of *Libertà*. Meanwhile dictated for the same journal a brief letter of reply to the *Unità*, the organ of the Naples Communists, and so disposed of its threats by telling an appropriate anecdote which made every one laugh including themselves.[22]

[22] The Communist weekly in Naples had printed an old phrase of Marx's that 'the weapons of criticism' should be substituted by the phrase 'the criticism of weapons,' and my little letter, to which I refer above, was as follows:—

Sorrento, April 2nd, 1944.

Dear Friends,

The paragraphs with which *Libertà* decided to reply to you, for reasons which were not at all objective or in the service of truth, were, to be exact, written in the office when I was far from Naples. I was told about it after it was done. This does not prevent my approving it in every syllable. But do you know what I would have said if I had had to reply?

The phrase used by me 'the weapons of criticism' which you say should be met by the phrase 'the criticism of weapons,' in fact, by violence, reminds me at once of an anecdote. The story is of an officer who was dancing in a drawing-room, when a gentleman whispered to his neighbour: "How badly that officer dances!" The brave officer, having heard these words, came when

April 2nd

Slightly better to-day so that I was able to write a brief essay on the æsthetics of Winckelmann. But I had hardly finished it when Morelli arrived to inform me of a sudden change upon the political scene. An Italian Communist has arrived from Russia with the conventional name of Hercules, real name Togliatti. He has convoked the Communists and exhorted them and the other Parties to collaborate with Badoglio's Government, overriding the question of the King's abdication, and to concentrate everything on the war against the Germans. He has declared that the Communists would straightaway collaborate. This is certainly an able shot aimed by the Soviet Republic against the Anglo-Americans, for in this way, under the guise of intensifying the war effort against the Germans, the Communists are introduced into the Government. There they can start new policies over and above or against the other Parties, who will be constrained to follow them while the Communists will feel no embarrassment whatever about the pact which they once signed together with all the Parties and the Committee of Liberation, nor indeed will they care about that very recent meeting in which they joined up with Socialists and the Party of Action to protest against Churchill, clamouring for the abdication of the King, the exclusion of all members of the house of Savoy, and for a Republic! I have already several times warned Omodeo, but in vain, of the dangerous game being played by the Action Party in supporting the Communists, who themselves have no scruples about any binding pacts. And if the Communists now start collaborating with Badoglio and the King, what will the other Parties do, and particularly the Christian Democrats, who also have their 'masses' and who will not wish to stay out of the Government, leaving the camp free to the Communists? So we have hurried on what was already decided: to publish the details of De Nicola's negotiations with the King, which were made with the approval of the Liberals, and to publish the

he had finished the dance and planted himself squarely in front of the civilian and said: "Sir, you should know that, if I dance badly, I fight well!"

What did the good civilian reply? He did not lose his presence of mind or his logic. He said just this: "Then you should always fight, and never dance!"

You may threaten or cause violence if you like, but leave dialectics, idealism, materialism and philosophy alone.

Such a reply may seem to lack the gravity suitable to a philosopher, but we are all in Naples where one may still laugh; we are all, I won't say Communists, but among Communists, and I know many of them and apart from fierce newspaper polemics I have always found them people of good sense and good manners.

Yours etc.,

King's undertaking to retire. Thus, on the basis upon which the Communists now want to start working, we substitute a clearly superior action, which does not skirt round the question but resolves the question of the person of the King: moreover, it will win the consent of all the Parties and of the Communists themselves. De Nicola has seen Sforza and to-morrow they will come back here together to take the next steps. The blame for what is happening or for what was about to happen must rest entirely with the Anglo-American politicians, the Churchills, the Edens and the Roosevelts, who have for months turned down the reasonable and most reasoned proposals and wishes of the Italian Liberals and Democrats, who asked that the King should be removed so that a Democratic Government might be formed. But I have observed and experienced that the English and the Americans who manage political affairs in Naples are very slow in understanding. Nor did they understand this time what was immediately evident to us all, that the order to the Communists to collaborate with the King was directed against the Anglo-Americans, but they had actually decided that the Communist Order of the Day should be favourably commented on by *Risorgimento*! They ask it to be neutral and Del Secolo needed a lot of persuasion to publish it, but he made no political comment.

April 3rd

Onorato and Carlo Croce unexpectedly arrived in the afternoon, having been given a permit to travel and furnished with a distinctive pass, in answer to a request from me. But the Allied authorities had not told me they had granted it. What horrors they told me of the destruction of villages and the massacre of the people, not to mention the looting by the Germans in those regions of the Abruzzo! Montenerodomo has been razed to the ground; on the neighbouring properties the peasants' houses are destroyed, the peasants are scattered or have fled into other provinces and the cattle have been slaughtered or carried away. My own nephews hid in the woods for two months so as not to be taken and transported to Germany. As the dangers increased they decided to flee and reach British occupied territory, and ten members of the family, men, women and children, walked for eight days through German machine-gun fire and mined districts. One of the sisters, Elisa, was killed when a mine exploded. They had to leave her in the open country where she fell, being unable to transport her owing to the machine-gun fire. They have taken refuge in the house of two old aunts at San Martino in Pensilis, having nothing but the clothes they are wearing. People of Abruzzo, in the places where they passed through, were wonderfully kind and gave all the help they could, depriving themselves of their own poor reserves. Now my nephews are trying to find some work in order to support their sisters and nephews.

April 4th

The day passed mainly with De Nicola and Sforza planning the meeting of the Junta of the Party, nominated by the Bari Congress, which will be held here, since I cannot go to Naples. Rodinò and Togliatti, the trusted envoy of Communism, will come. I shall read them a declaration we have all three written to announce the King's decision to withdraw and to entrust the Lieutenant-Generalcy of the realm to the Prince of Piedmont: a decision which the King is prepared to have published immediately, although the transfer of powers to the Lieutenant-General will be deferred until after the liberation of Rome, which latter point meets with certain reservations on our part. Omodeo arrived, having taken part yesterday, together with the other members of the Committee of Liberation, in the meeting of the Junta in Naples, Togliatti being present. Omodeo spoke firmly against the proposal to collaborate with the King and with Badoglio, and against the breaking up of the six-party collaboration. His speech was not without effect even on Togliatti.

April 5th

Morelli, Bergami and Cassandro brought me the refusal of the Liberal, Christian Democrat and Labour Democrat Parties to collaborate with Badoglio's royal Government. They also gave me useful information for the meeting of the Junta to-morrow in my house, and we exchanged ideas and suggestions about the future course of affairs.

April 6th

The Junta nominated by the Bari Congress met in my study in the afternoon with Sforza, Rodinò and Togliatti, as well as myself present. Togliatti reminded me of Turin in 1920 and of the group of young university men to whom he belonged and whom I knew, and of several of them who have turned to Communism or to philo-

Communism, and of Gramsci, who stood out among them all, of Gobetti, and of a visit which I paid to their communistic newspaper, *L'Ordime nuovo*, where I had an appointment with Gobetti and found him ready for anything, with the barricades already up and other military precautions taken. Del Secolo also came to Sorrento with some Anglo-American journalists, also Morelli and Cassandro, but they waited for news in the room next door. I read out the declaration which De Nicola and Sforza and I had agreed upon,[23] and I opened the discussion with it. Despite the lack of understanding on the part of some of them I succeeded in getting our work acknowledged and a vote in favour of an immediate Lieutenant-Generalcy, without waiting for the liberation of Rome. Togliatti was among the first to approve the result of our work, nor did he offer any objection or make any difficulties. A step forward was thus achieved, but what is to follow appears to be full of uncertainty and peril. Now we must make the Allied authorities, and especially the English, understand that new obstacles must not be set to our work, which could only damage them and us.

April 7th

Visit from a lawyer who lives on this Sorrento peninsular, who has spent recent years in America, in Belgium and in France and, having two sons fighting in Spain with the Republicans when he finally came back to Italy from France, had been sent to 'confino' on the Islands. He gave me a most vivid and detailed picture of Spanish affairs, with special emphasis on the disintegrating activities of the Communist Party. Previously that Party had not existed in Spain. In Catalonia there had been the so-called Anarchists, who in fact were good administrators. Wherever the Communist Party had taken root, with subtle and at the same time violent action, a few groups had been able to get control of branches of the Administration, providing themselves with the semblance of a political following by means of favours and menaces or by excluding people from the enjoyment of the necessities of life. Immediately after their defeat the Communists vanished and to-day in Spain there is not a trace of them. My interlocutor fears that they may get control of Italy in the same way.

[23] *Per la nuova vita dell'Italia*, pp. 71–2.

April 8th

Morelli, Cassandro, Calvi and later Sforza and Tarchiani came from Naples, not to mention those who came with Easter wishes and stayed to talk politics. Every one is talking of the impression made by the Communist attempt in Naples to take over the management of Italian political affairs, and of the crowds who rush to join that Party: black-coated workers, officers, fishes out of water, ex-Fascists, etc. Another period of Fascism for Italy is feared, if Communism means Bolshevism, and the latter refrains from justifying itself politically by the economic revolution, and only justifies itself by its politically totalitarian regime. How Mussolini imitated the Russian example by applying Russian political methods while being most accommodating in economic matters, satisfying first one and then another! The awful thing is that after twenty years of longing for freedom and the expansion of spiritual forces which freedom allows, we might by devious turns lose our liberty again. In the evening Tarchiani, who has seen Berneri's widow, spoke of her version of the assassination of the Rosselli brothers by the Spanish Communists, saying that he excluded it, for he followed all the inquiries which were made at the time in France. He says that the crime was Mussolini's work and that he used persons affiliated to a reactionary French sect, paid by him, so that they should remove this much feared anti-Fascist, who was hated for the whole of his past, for his activities in France among the exiles, and for his recent participation in the Spanish war.[24]

April 9th

Discussed the situation at length with Sforza and expressed the view that Sforza should not object to the continuance of Badoglio in office if he were surrounded by a Ministry composed of Party representatives. His continuance in office may become necessary if the Allies, having accepted the withdrawal of the King and a Lieutenant-Generalcy, should persist in asking that Badoglio, with whom they signed the armistice, should remain; yet on the other hand this would be a provisional expedient, because once in Rome Badoglio will have to give way to another Prime Minister. Sforza recognized the justice of my remarks. I recommended that in considering the composition of the new Ministry, the institution of a

[24] Since then the documents and the revelations which have come to light after the German defeat have fully confirmed Tarchiani's version.

consultative assembly should be kept in mind, a body which can discuss regulations and to whom an account of the country's finances can be presented : in this way, in as many matters as possible, some kind of public control can straightaway be exercised again. In the afternoon Max Salvadori (Sylvester) told me that the English representatives of the Allies in Naples acknowledge that they have made a great mistake in supporting the King and in closing their ears to our demands and now feel in a serious fix on account of the Communist peril which throws its shadow before. So they are prepared to bring immediate pressure upon the King so that he should withdraw, appoint the Lieutenant-General and allow the formation of a Ministry composed of the Parties; but they still cling to Badoglio for the above-mentioned reasons. If we were to accept Badoglio, an obstacle would be removed and they might agree to the solution we propose. All this should occur within the next four or five days, because events are precipitating and present perils must be avoided. Sforza and Tarchiani called and the conversation went on between the four of us. At first Sforza renewed his repugnance at any collaboration with Badoglio and believed that we must not tarnish ourselves with such a contact but preserve ourselves for the future. He said that the Allies must be persuaded to abandon Badoglio and that he should only be accepted in an extreme emergency. But six months were necessary for persuading the Americans and the British that the King must withdraw, and at least another whole month would be required to induce them to give up Badoglio. It is important, too, not to increase unreasonably the number of those who are opposed to the present Government and not to go against the expectations of temperate persons, who ask for a compromise solution and would not forgive us if, by refusing again, we should render the much desired revival of Italy impossible. Tarchiani, who is said to give diehard advice to Sforza, completely agreed with me and realized that one must bow to political necessity, or, as he put it, one must sometimes be ready to lose popularity. Sforza ended by consenting, saying that he did it only to please me, and I replied that I could in no way accept his declaration, because our discussion had shown that we had all equally submitted to the logic of the situation, which is what it is. Salvadori undertook to refer our conclusions back to the Allied authorities, to go with their representatives to Salerno to-morrow and to let us know what happens.

April 10th

Sforza and Tarchiani have gone away again. In the afternoon several people, who must have heard about the whole question, came from Naples to tell me that it would be an absolute disgrace to join forces with Badoglio. I asked them what other course they could propose and they said that we must insist with the Allies that they abandon their intentions; but they then admitted that such an attempt, whose result anyway would be doubtful, would need a good deal of time. Told Morelli, Cassandro and Calvi of Sforza's decision to accept Badoglio again, whom he had already proposed as Regent, when the Regency question was under discussion. Then we spoke of the possible complications of the Cabinet, a painful argument to me, as is anything connected with the preferment or the exclusion of persons. I urged the beginning of conversations about the Cabinet with the Party representatives and told them to discuss it with Sforza, while I would discuss it with Rodinò. A rough sketch of the Ministry was made, in such a way as not to necessitate a crisis, once Rome is reached, it then being only necessary to fill the gap, which for the present would be covered by *interim* office holders, and perhaps to make a few changes.

April 11th

Unconfirmed news that the Allies are bringing pressure on the King to establish the Lieutenant-Generalcy straightaway. The Allies cling to Badoglio, but would agree to De Nicola in his place, if the latter would accept (which I doubt). They recognize that in any case Badoglio would have to form a completely new Ministry with the advice of the Parties. They admit and increasingly deplore the mistakes of their policy toward Italy in not having welcomed the wishes of the Liberal, but they say that they cannot interfere any more in our internal affairs, if Italian liberty is to be respected. This would be a curious scruple were it not tainted with hypocrisy, since they have, up to the present, supported the King against the manifest feeling of Italians; but perhaps they really are afraid of displeasing Russia by cutting across the line which Russia has taken in Italy through the Communists. I received a letter from Sforza; he has had a long conversation with De Nicola, who also sees no absolute objection to accepting a Badoglio premiership, but De Nicola advised Sforza against taking the Ministry of Foreign Affairs, since nothing useful can be achieved there for the present, and Sforza would only 'diminish himself.' De Nicola spoke however of the importance of the Ministry of Interior. Sforza has really always told me of his wish to be Foreign Minister, of this being the real field for his activities, but if he has now changed his mind, I will certainly not put obstacles in his path. I hear from Naples that the Action Party alone will refuse to go in with Badoglio, and with this refusal seeks to become the pivot of all the opposition in Italy. But this is pure folly!

April 12th

I had hardly got up and gone to my study when Arangio Ruiz came to tell me that the Anglo-Americans have brought pressure on the King to establish his son as Lieutenant-General immediately, but that the King resisted and ended by saying that he would do it only if he could add these words to the proclamation: "Owing to the pressure put upon me by the Allied Powers." At this point the Allied authorities retreated. Arangio Ruiz showed me a summary of the King's proclamation which should have been published this morning, but which has been suspended for a few hours as Duke Acquarone begged Arangio Ruiz to let me read it first and to ask me what modifications I would suggest. I made some alterations, the vital one that "the King will maintain the Lieutenant-Generalcy during the period of hostilities and until the day on which the whole Italian people can decide what form of State they desire"; and I reminded him that this proviso had been communicated to us by the King through De Nicola and that it had been repeatedly promised by the Allied Powers. I added that I firmly supported the demands for an immediate Lieutenant-Generalcy and that my suggestions, modifying the programme, were dictated solely by a desire to avoid bitterness or complications in the questions under discussion. Arangio Ruiz left again immediately, carrying my alterations with him to Salerno. He said that Badoglio wanted to talk to me and would come in a day or two, as he was now suffering from rheumatism, and I let Sforza know about this forthcoming visit.

April 13th

A visit from Minifie accompanied by another American journalist and a lady journalist who is supposed to have a good reputation and is certainly an intelligent person and understands Italian affairs. I explained to them all how slow the Allied authorities are in understanding us and our needs, and how damaging to them and to us when they finally see that we were right and then welcome our proposals with great delay. I gave them several examples of this. In the afternoon many friends came: first, Altavilla and Ugo Forti, who said Badoglio would come to-morrow morning to confer with me. Discussed the composition of the Cabinet in detail with Rodinò: a serious difficulty is that all the six Parties must share the posts equally, though some of them can only produce completely insignificant men. Rodinò, who was formerly Secretary for War, explained how, from his own experience, he was convinced that the Cabinet could not possibly be formed under such conditions. He spoke of the need to make Arangio Ruiz Minister of Education, because Omodeo has used such violent and sarcastic invective against the Catholics as to have made himself disliked throughout his Party. I admitted the truth of this but I replied that Omodeo has given evidence of possessing all the qualities and virtues necessary for a good Minister of Education and that, moreover, he is the only capable man whom the Action Party can provide, and this apart from the very strong political and personal reasons which I have for not letting him be sacrificed to Catholic aversion. We agreed that the Christian Democrats will have their Under-Secretary in the Ministry of Education, as will the other Party, coupling opponents, because such is the law of the Ministries, absurd as it is, *ex aequo,* and I only turned down one name he proposed, that of a too combative Catholic. To-morrow morning I will have a taste of Badoglio's disposition. In the afternoon Sforza will come and I shall discuss a vital question with him: whether he would not agree to serve like me as a Minister without portfolio. Thus I think I have seven or eight days' work before me, for a decision can hardly be reached sooner. I have at last been able to read the King's proclamation, which I could not hear on the wireless. What on earth has happened? Not only does it not contain the modifications I was asked for and sent, but the form of the proclamation is completely different to the one I was given to read, and is strangely illogical, because the King establishes a Lieutenant-Generalcy *sine die* and announces that he is withdrawing to live a private life. But of whom then is the Lieutenant-General a Lieutenant-General—of a King who is no longer King? And if the Lieutenant-General is ill or dies, or gets tired and resigns, who nominates the new Lieutenant-General of the King who is no longer King? All told, I understand very little of all this, perhaps because, faced with this accomplished fact, the effort to understand is not worth while, since the deed is done. (De Nicola came at 4 p.m. and told me that I could write these facts in my diary as certain: that on the 10th at 11 a.m. the King received a visit from the Allied authorities, who requested an audience under some pretext, but kept the real object of their visit dark. They brought pressure to bear on him to relinquish his powers. The following day, the 11th, they came back and proposed an additional paragraph to the proclamation about withdrawing from public life and that what was said about fighting by the side of the United Nations should come out or be watered down. The King accepted the first request but nobly refused the second. Hence the queerness of this Lieutenant-Generalcy, in which the situation and the character of nominator and lieutenant are altered, is entirely due to the juridical wisdom of the Anglo-American authorities and of their 'experts').

Sorrento, April 14th

Collected my thoughts this morning for the expected visit of Badoglio, who came about 9.30 a.m. and stayed for an hour and a half. It was a fairly cordial conversation, during which I had to be extremely careful several times to keep watch, because I was filled with sympathy for this old soldier, who, despite his errors and his faults, liberated Italy from Mussolini on July 25th and faced grave peril and even an attempted assassination during the following weeks. I quickly reached agreement with him that the Cabinet must be completely renewed except for keeping on the military collaborators and eventually certain technical people who were not compromised under Fascism. After we have agreed on the Cabinet and have sent him the names and apportioned the Ministries and the Under-Secretaries, he will put his resignation and that of his Cabinet in the hands of the King and will accept the King's instructions to stay in office. We exchanged opinions on certain names, but I told him that mine were quite personal views and that my conclusions might be confirmed or substituted by others after conversations among the Parties. Generally speaking, I found him friendly. He has already been in touch with various Parties, if I understood rightly, except the Party of Action. And since the latter is very closely connected with Sforza, the question again is, what will Sforza do? He is no longer interested in being Foreign Minister, although he had constantly had this post in mind, but on the other hand Badoglio told me that the Allies do not think much of him, especially as recently, in the course of much argument and invective, he called Churchill 'a sparrow.'[25] Badoglio asked me whether Sforza still wanted the Ministry of the Interior, or whether he would be prepared to enter the Cabinet as a Minister without portfolio, and I replied that I would know the answer to-day, as Sforza was coming to lunch. We agreed about other questions, such as the exercise of some sort of control, especially financial control, on the Government, and to that end, despite the many practical difficulties, to form a consultative assembly. We also agreed on an epuration Commission, and that Zanibomi should be given some other job more suitable to him. As for Einaudi, who is wanted as Minister of Finance, Badoglio said that he had been trying these last five months to get him back to Italy from Switzerland, indeed to Naples, but that the undertaking was too dangerous. Other difficulties prevent our having Federico Ricci, who is in Genoa. We have made another appointment for Tuesday morning here unless I telephone him Monday to ask for a deferment. Then Sforza and Tarchiani came. I had a long conversation with the former alone, and later Tarchiani came in and we all decided that Sforza was prepared to join the Ministry as a Minister without portfolio, for he realized that to stay outside it with the Action Party would in fact amount to opposing and weakening the Democratic Cabinet for which every one is asking, and which is necessary. He tells me that he will confirm his decision to-morrow. When Badoglio asked me what office I would prefer I replied that I certainly could not keep out of the Cabinet, because if I did, however friendly and loyal my attitude, I should be accused of certain feelings, or criticisms of mine would be invented, which were not favourable to this or that government, and I therefore replied that, since I could not shoulder any administrative office, I would enter the Cabinet as a Minister without portfolio in order to share responsibility with the Government. As Badoglio hopes that De Nicola will enter the Government in a similar way, I begged him to work for this personally, and I asked Sforza to do likewise. In the evening Morelli came and I showed him a list of probable Ministers: however, there is not so much cloth to be cut and every Party has to be satisfied, even if it has not many capable or expert men available. Still, I hope that, by and

[25] '*Testa di passerotto*' is the phrase, literally 'sparrow's head,' implying feather-brained. Since then, Count Sforza and Mr. Churchill have had tea together in London in 1948 and made friends. Tr.

large, we shall collect a Cabinet that is not too bad; it will certainly be superior to the present one.

April 15th

Badoglio told me yesterday that it is not true that Italy made an unconditional surrender, as announced by the Allied Powers, but that an armistice containing certain negotiated clauses was made. He told me that he was working to shelve the word 'cobelligerency' (a word which the Anglo-Americans want to use and which signifies nothing) and to achieve the declaration of an Alliance: to that end the formation of a democratic Ministry will be most helpful. He also told me of the sad days in September. To-day I was able to rest by burying myself in new literary labours. The Mayor of Sorrento, De Angelis (whom I know through literary exchanges, and because he is the grandson of the folklore writer, Amalfi, a favourite scholar of Vittorio Imbriani), came to ask my opinion on two proposed inscriptions for the house in Sorrento where Roberto Bracco died last year. I chose the shortest, which is simple and affectionate, and turned down the other one, which was pompous and inaccurate, and then I asked who had written them, and found that the first had been written by himself and the second had come from Naples. In the afternoon Sforza returned to say he had agreed to become a Minister without portfolio and said he felt comforted at the thought that De Nicola would do likewise, for he hopes or deludes himself that De Nicola will join us. I asked Sforza to try to come here to-morrow with De Nicola.

April 16th

In the morning, a few hours of literary work. Then visits and conversations. First came the two diplomats and counsellors of the Anglo-Americans in Naples, Rieber and Caccia, who came from General Macfarlane and asked me how the situation was moving, and I told them, with certain reserves. They let me understand that they much desired a happy solution to the present crisis, while protesting that they did not intend to interfere in any way or at any stage, out of respect for the freewill of the Italians. I said to them that the Italians had really helped themselves by getting the King to withdraw, and that we would have got out of the mess much more quickly if they had not been against this course. Then De Nicola visited me, still adamant to the new pressure I put upon him.[26] Then representatives of the Labour-Democrats (Bonomi's Party, as it is called here) came to express their wishes about the names to be included in the Cabinet. Then a host of Christian Democrats with friend Rodinò, with whom I had a painful encounter because he asked, in the name of the Party and of the Ecclesiastical authorities, that Omodeo should be excluded from the Ministry of Education; but I was firm and refused to admit interference from ecclesiastical authorities in the formation of a Government solely concerned with the national interest, and I drew their attention to the fact that the Christian Democrats were to hold the important Ministry of the Interior, and that therefore they should not try to arrange the other Ministries to suit themselves. Then I asked Rodinò and his followers, with all the others present, to set about perfecting the suggested list of Ministers with me, which I want to present after to-morrow to Badoglio, and thus we did for two hours, and worked with good results.

April 17th

Early this morning the good Brindisi came from Capri to tell me of what a most zealous Mayor in the island is doing, and suddenly, in the midst of the talk, he told me that he had heard on the ship coming from Capri that Gentile had been murdered in Florence! The news unfortunately has been confirmed by the B.B.C. This is the end of a man with whom I worked for thirty years and with whom I have always been sincerely friendly, affectionate and loyal. I broke off relations with him when he passed over to Fascism, a step which was the more serious because of the contamination which he allowed philosophy to receive from Fascism. That is why I never ceased in the pages of *Critica* to contest and restate many of the things which he would assert to the besmirching of truth. But although I felt the break between us to be complete, and on the other hand, was certain that somehow the artificial and lying edifice of Fascism would crumble, I thought that in such a future it would fall to me, for the sake of a youthful friendship, to provide at least for his personal safety and to make life tolerable for him, by calling him back to the studies which he had deserted. Last August already, I was grieved by a letter of reproach which the new Minister of

[26] For details given to me by De Nicola in those days about the way in which the King's proclamation was dictated, see entries in this diary under April 13th.

Education had openly addressed to him and I recommended a more temperate procedure, such as getting a common friend to advise him to anticipate his retirement, which was due anyway, by spontaneously asking to be retired. Then happened what happened: Italy was cut in half. I knew that he had accepted the Presidency of the Italian Academy and was very prominent in the Fascist Republic, making speeches in its taste, of which I was given some of the most violent extracts. Nothing is known either of the perpetrators or of the circumstances of his death, but the B.B.C., who defined it as 'justice' and added severe comments on the man, made Adelina burst into tears as she was listening, for she remembered him in the early days of our marriage as a good natured man and a friend whom we welcomed festively when he used to come and stay with us in Naples. Sforza and other friends came to Naples informing me of the attitude of the everlasting Party of Action and of its negotiations with the Communists and the Socialists against collaboration with Badoglio: its representatives have not shown up here, even though I insisted painfully, with an old and valued friend like Rodinò, that a post should be reserved for that Party in the person of Omodeo, who is the only man they have with enough capacity to be the Minister of Education. Neither Sforza nor the others from Naples were able to produce any concrete political suggestions which could usefully advance the work undertaken. So here I am, faced with direct agreement with Badoglio, with a view to preserving as best we can a Liberal development of Italian affairs. I feel as though I were crushed by the weight of it, and I complain to myself that I did not deserve labours so contrary to my temperament, my ability and my whole life, which has been that of a scholar. Nevertheless, I cannot withdraw and leave others to do this task, because I find no one round me who has either the will, the strength or the authority to undertake it. For my whole thought is the good of Italy together with a certain natural common sense and a certain broadmindedness which may usefully serve the essential goal, in fact to prove that we Italians, as we have announced, know how to make a Democratic Government against the Royal Government. So to-morrow I shall hear Badoglio again.

April 18th

Things went much better and much more smoothly than I feared yesterday and in little more than an hour we drew up the first outline of a Ministry. I proposed, and Badoglio accepted, that Tarchiani be Under-Secretary for War. I got him to accept Omodeo for Education, even though Badoglio (at whom the Christian Democrats have certainly been getting) asked me whether I insisted; to which I replied, "Yes, for many reasons." There was already agreement about Arangio Ruiz as Minister for Justice. I begged him to take Renato Morelli as Under-Secretary to the Presidency, he, like the rest of us, elected by the Liberal group in the Committee of Liberation. The same group had at first wanted him to be Under-Secretary at the Ministry of the Interior so that Omodeo should not torment himself or me by thinking that Morelli (who is a sincere Catholic) would let himself be dominated by a Christian Democrat Minister of the Interior and thus drag the Liberals under. Badoglio also agreed to my proposal to give the Party of Action an Under-Secretaryship for the Interior. That Party so far refuses to collaborate and fusses about outside to form the nucleus of an inconclusive, impotent, and certainly (seeing the point which has now been reached) evil opposition. For Agriculture and Food I proposed one of Bonomi's Labour Democrats, with Bergami as Under-Secretary, a most competent and active man. Meanwhile Rodinò is giving up the Ministry of the Interior to some other member of his Party, and he too wants to enter the Cabinet as a Minister without portfolio, which does not displease me, as we shall then be three—Sforza, he and I—all three colleagues in Giolitti's last Ministry, a triad of old politicians which will, as it were, hold the new Cabinet baby at its baptism and supply a little experience and counsel to the relatively young and untried Ministers. Morelli and Calvi, who came to receive my instructions, saw the Cabinet scheme and judged it good except for the allotment of the Ministry for Industry to the Communists, about which Calvi (who has come from Rome and acts as spokesman for the anti-Fascists in the capital) says that it is an appointment which will dismay and diminish the confidence of the industrialists in northern Italy, not only the big ones, but the smaller ones too. I will write about this to Badoglio to-morrow, although it seems difficult for him, once he has made an undertaking, to go back on it, I think.

April 19th

Worked in the early hours, as I did in the last hours of yesterday, on the revision of my volumes which are to be reprinted. Michail

Kostylev, representative with the Italian Government of the Government of the Union of Soviet Republics, came to see me together with Alexander Bogomolov, Ambassador and plenipotentiary of the Union. We spoke of Italian and non-Italian policy and I explained to them, at the risk of seeming ingenuous, 'what Liberalism really is,' and I said that I knew very well that they did not allow it, but that sooner or later they will have to do so even in Russia, and that if peace and civilization are to be re-established that would be the only possible way. Badoglio has written to me that he would like to give the Ministry of Agriculture to a Socialist and I have drawn his attention to the fact that Socialists and Communists are all one and that it would be dangerous and would not please the other Parties if all the economic Ministries were given to these two Parties. I said it would be especially dangerous in the Food Department, where partisan distribution is to be feared. But from his reply I think he has already consented to the request made to him (matters were remedied by appointing Bergami as Under-Secretary for Food). Originally, I had suggested merging the Ministries of Industry and Labour under Piccardi, who is notoriously generous in favouring the workers at the expense of the industrialists, but Badoglio will not hear of it on account of Piccardi's attitude towards him when he was in Badoglio's Royal Government. I expected news from Naples; but Morelli, Cassandro and Calvi came to tell me that everything is in a state of confusion and excitement there, and that the members of the Socialist, Communist and Action Parties go on trying to torpedo any collaboration with Badoglio and there is reason to believe that they are trying to push the other three Parties into a Ministry by themselves, so as to be able to shout afterwards that the Ministry is a reactionary one and so launch the Opposition against it. But in reality, the very factious brains in the Party of Action are hoping for this in vain, because there will be a majority anyhow of five to one, or at the worst of four to two. Omodeo came, then Raimondo with Tarchiani, all of them on the offensive, Raimondo timidly, Omodeo timidly and discreetly because he knew of my well-weighed decision, but Tarchiani fairly bursting forth (he has just joined the Action Party, I think in order to stay near his personal friends). The purpose of the assault was to force me to accept the Premiership, which Sforza cannot do, and so take the place of Badoglio. Some employee of his administration has criticized some of the administration's actions and the Allies, who want Badoglio, have stupidly and to his discredit let these things be published (probably without even thinking about the significance or the veracity of the criticism), and my visitors think that therefore the Allies no longer support Badoglio and it would be easy to rule him out. The odd thing is that I am offered the Presidential crown by that very Action Party to which I have always given its deserts, in speech and writing, and which has repaid me with dislike, although always with respect. Now it is bustling to get something out of me, which in my opinion would be politically disastrous for Italy and dishonourable for me, since Badoglio has put his trust in me and I have received the consent of Tarchiani and of Sforza, and also because I have given Badoglio advice and made certain undertakings from the beginning of our negotiations. Naturally I refused the offer, telling them as much as I could, and in the end they trampled on my words, shouting that I preferred contaminating myself (for they used this big word to imply that I would become 'impure' by going near Badoglio) to forming a Ministry. In fact I had chosen not to remain a statue of purity alongside the wonderfully pure marble statue of the Party of Action, for what was at stake was the integrity of Italy. That Badoglio should have accepted the Premiership was fully justified, not only because here in Naples we have no other suitable person and the Allies have always had confidence in him (nor can one lightly believe that they have lost it, especially as a British officer came to me the other day to ask my advice about that publication mentioned above, made by the Allies, saying that they feared they had committed a *gaffe,* nor is it their first) but also because Badoglio is an excellent military man, has the war effort in hand and has already sent twelve battalions to the Front to fight the Germans, and is getting others ready. Who can lightly interrupt such labours or interrupt his constantly pursued objective, to which I think he is nearing, to pass from co-belligerency to alliance? I trembled with anger at the injury to myself which I see in this attempt which, though subconsciously, presupposes low personal ambitions which I have not got, or at best thinks that I would be capable, after much praise, of shameless behaviour. I have decided to go to Naples to-morrow to see how things are. Badoglio has invited me and made an appointment for me to-morrow at 10 o'clock.

Naples, April 20th

At eight o'clock left Sorrento with Max Salvadori, who took me to Naples in a car with Elena. I went immediately to the Palace of the Military Command, where Cassandro and Calvi, who were waiting for me, told me that the Action Party last night voted definitely against any collaboration with Badoglio, and that the Socialists, one does not know from what motives, have taken the same attitude. A few minutes later Badoglio arrived and I gave him this news, and he said (and I knew already through another channel that this would happen) that he had received a visit from General Macfarlane urging him to hurry the Ministry forward as the Allies could not go on much longer without Italian Ministers with whom to deal. If on our part a little more time may be allowed, I think also that, after the negotiations and agreements of the last few days, it is now time to make the Cabinet, and quickly. Badoglio would like to finish to-day or to-morrow. Since the Communists are for collaboration, we are already in a majority of four to two; Badoglio said it was five to two, because he would like to include the representative of the Liberal Democratic Party, which had so much following and importance before the advent of Fascism, but I pointed out that majority and minority must be exclusively calculated among the six Parties of the Committee of Liberation, and we would only be five if the Socialists remain loyal. Then he asked me whether Sforza still proposed to collaborate and I reassured him about this, and to make doubly sure I had Sforza rung up and said I would go to see him. Although the Action Party, of which he is not a member but to which he is attached by many personal ties, obstinately refuses to collaborate, Sforza confirmed his own undertaking to work with us. Back at the Command headquarters I learnt that the Socialists, too, are collaborating. Rodinò and the Christian Democrats are with us in wishing to revise the allotment of the economic Ministries, but in subsequent conversation agreed with Badoglio's declaration, already made to me, that the new Ministry must put the war first, followed by epuration, supplies, restoration of communications, transport and ordinary administration, and not attend to political, administrative or economic reforms until Italy is liberated and there can be elections and a Parliament once more. Thus, he says, Party colours have no importance under present conditions. The Communists and Socialists arrived and proposed another Minister without portfolio, in the person of Zaniboni, and when I observed that I had seen from their press that he had been expelled from their Party, they replied that this was 'an old affair' (i.e. of four weeks old!). Then they proposed the lawyer Mancini, from Cosenza, instead of Zaniboni and we ended by agreeing, although the character of a Minister without portfolio, which should be that of an elder statesman, has thus been travestied. The Communists said that two Liberal Under-Secretaries would not be welcome to the members of their Party (or to their clients, as Reale and Togliatti afterwards confessed to me in private conversation); but they were vigorously contradicted and the matter was dropped. Then I went to Sforza's house, where we discussed some of the appointments; it seemed especially deplorable that the candidates first put forward by the Socialists, and those supported to-day by the Communists, are minor figures, and that the heads of the Parties do not want to go into the Government. In the evening I heard that the Party of Action, after a further meeting, had withdrawn its previous decision. Thus finally, the first democratic Ministry since the fall of Fascism has been made; if it had not been achieved great discredit would have fallen upon Italy.

April 21st

Omodeo came early, very excited, tempestuously insisting that the Cabinet had been made without any 'invitation' to the Party of Action and that this Party alone 'had preserved its dignity' by keeping its distance, and that now everything was in jeopardy again, unless the objections of the Action Party about under-secretaries were accepted; if not, they would not participate. I replied that there had been no agreement among the other five Parties; that each one had negotiated with Badoglio through its own representatives, which is the duty of heads of Parties; that the Liberal Party had not even had to send any one to Badoglio, because he had come to me; that I had left three empty places for the Party of Action, just as to the others and as important as the places allotted to the Liberals, i.e. the Ministry of Education, for which I had suggested Omodeo, and two Under-Secretaryships at the Interior and at the Treasury. I laughingly said to him that his Party was behaving like the guest who arrived two hours late for lunch and, although the dishes had been put aside, wanted the others to sit down and begin eating all over again. I concluded that for to-day I could do no more than urge the representatives of my Party, who would be attending instead of me, to support the request of the Action Party, and I said I thought that Badoglio would be good-natured and accommodating, but that he (Omodeo) must get it firmly fixed in his mind that the discussion was not one between the Party of

Action and the other Parties, but between them and Badoglio. The Action Party's unconsidered refusal to collaborate with Badoglio had resulted in an undertaking by the other five Parties, together with the Ministers without portfolio, to participate as a majority of five to one, and none of us could go back on this undertaking. (It is ironical that the paper *L'Azione,* the organ of the Action Party in Naples, came out to-day, April 21st, carrying the order of the day presented by that Party in the Junta, which designates me, unasked and unconsenting, as an alternative Prime Minister to Badoglio. If they have no other guardian angel to watch over them, heaven help them!) When my friend Omodeo's excitement had cooled a little, I sent Cassandro and Calvi to talk with Badoglio. In Sforza's house I gradually received news of the latest negotiations and of minor changes. The Communists were forced to abandon their attempt to keep their leaders on ice and Togliatti received a fifth Ministership without portfolio. Badoglio gave way, as I foresaw, about the Liberal Democratic Party representative and withdrew one Under-Secretaryship from the Party of Action, but formed a new Ministry (of Public Works) for them and gave it to Tarchiani. I am pleased, because in this way another estimable and intelligent man has entered the Cabinet. Thus in the afternoon Badoglio was able to tell the journalists that the new Ministry had been formed. During the afternoon and throughout the evening a succession of visitors for me in Sforza's house, where I am staying, and I have to keep talking. But generally speaking, a sense of relief and a general satisfaction has taken the place of the ill-temper of the past few days. In truth, the formation of a Ministry like this one was exceedingly difficult and painful. It is illogical too, since a political organ has had to be made from six different, hostile and unequally strong Parties, and it is stretching many points to treat them all alike and give them an equal number of representatives. Fortune has been good to us in these first steps: let us hope it will assist us in the next stages. As I went into Sforza's house I asked the friends who came with me whether there was a shelter in the house; when asked why I had made this unusual inquiry, I replied "because I fear that the heavens will strike us to-night for our sin against nature, and will send us an air-raid." And the air-raid alarm and the anti-aircraft fire did come, just as I was going to sit down to dinner with Sforza's son at about 9 p.m., and I was in fact forced to go down to the shelter, where I found several people I knew and where we talked. But since I dress very slowly, as I have not yet the complete use of my left arm, and because the gun-fire was intermittent, I slept half-clothed and therefore little and badly.

Sorrento, April 22nd

Got up at six, wrote the notes of this diary for the last few days. Then went with Renato Morelli and Parente on a long over-due visit of thanks to De Nicola for his extremely important contribution, without which this Cabinet would have lacked its necessary premiss. De Nicola was much moved and his eyes filled with tears; he said that the Cabinet we had made was as good as it could be, given the conditions, although the irrational and mechanical manner in which it had been put together were not exemplary. In this I fully agree with him. We discussed various aspects of the new political situation in which we now find ourselves. De Nicola was grieved that we Liberals had objected to the inclusion of a highly respected name suggested by him, of a member of the Liberal Democratic Party, Rubilli. The truth is we Liberals did agree, but the Party of Action representatives were against, and Badoglio, in the general euphoria of having formed the Ministry, gave them that little plum. The Democratic Liberal Party is to blame, for it did not get itself recognized in August 1943 by the Committee of Liberation in Rome, and later it got involved with the politicians who supported the King's Government in Brindisi. Returned to Sorrento where I felt tired, but after resting on the sofa I recovered and put some order among my papers. Klaus Mann, the son of Thomas, came to see me and we exchanged news about common friends. I asked him to send my greetings to his father, when he writes. I had had no news of him for several years.

April 24th

The car came from Salerno to fetch me at 8 a.m. and by 10 a.m. many of the Ministers and Under-Secretaries were collected in the Communal Palace in Salerno. Those whom I did not know, especially the Service Ministers, were introduced to me. We had to delay for an hour and a half because Sforza and his friends telephoned from Naples to say that there was something wrong with their car. The Cabinet meeting was brief: agreement was reached about (1) a declaration of policy, which I and the other four Ministers without portfolio, will draw up at a meeting which is to take place in my house at 3.30 the day after to-morrow; (2) a declaration which Badoglio will read to the King, naming the Ministers nominated by the various Parties and the reasons why they are now united and in concord, which does not mean a renunciation by each one of their political beliefs. These will be propagated once the Italian people is allowed to meet freely and decide what kind of a State it wants. For the present they all equally feel that the good of the country must come first. Ideas were exchanged and agreement reached, especially about the convenience of having a consultative assembly alongside the Government, almost as a symbol of a not yet existing Parliament, and then the Cabinet broke up. At 2.30 p.m. all the Ministers left for Ravello, where the King received them all most correctly, and me cordially, with a vigorous handshake. I found him not only very old, as we, of his generation, have all become, but white in colour, flabby in his features and looking almost smaller than he already is, with fixed eyes. It seemed as though I had seen and yet not seen a face like that before, until I remembered that his mother, Queen Margherita, had become like that in expression, in her gestures and in attitude, when in 1921 I had occasion to visit her as Minister of Education. He listened to the formulas read out by Badoglio (which I think he had already seen before our arrival), and then read a few words saying that the good of the country had been his and Badoglio's aim and crowning thought. After we had signed the act of fealty he stayed behind to tell me that in the villa on the Sangro, where he lives, he had found many of my volumes and had found great interest in reading them, especially in my accounts of the lives of the Count of Campobasso Cola di Monforte and of Lucrezia d'Alagno. I suffered a good deal on account of the six or more hours' driving, and because of the very close day, and I went back to Sorrento with my stomach upset and feeling weak. In the evening we had to watch that excruciating spectacle of another German air-raid on Naples.

April 25th

Marquis Serra di Cassano came to tell me that the Prince of Piedmont wants to see me here to-morrow, and I said I was at his disposal, but sorry not to be able to go to see him, for reasons of health which he has fully understood. So he will come about 11 o'clock.

April 26th

In the morning drafted the Government's declaration of policy in my own way, so as to avoid a rudderless meeting with my four colleagues (like me without portfolios), which might produce a little monster if there is no text to accept or reject, to correct or revise, to lengthen or shorten. The Prince of Piedmont came at 11 a.m. and stayed with me for an hour. I told him my views on the present feeling against the Monarchy and how difficult was his personal position, and I demonstrated how useful it would be to make it quite clear, when he takes over the Lieutenant-Generalcy, that he has completely severed any relation with his past political attitude, which seemed to many a passive one. Further, I suggested he should entirely re-form his Court and choose men who were in easy relationship with the Democratic Parties. Suspicion of the men who surround him or who may yet surround him is pretty strong just now. He told me that for years and years every single move of his had been prevented or repressed by the men round his father. He spoke earnestly and with confidence of his historical studies and of the collections of fairly valuable documents which he had made on the history of Piedmont and of Naples. My impression to-day leaves me perplexed about the intelligence, the passions and the political vigour of the Prince. Then Sforza came and at 3 p.m. the other Ministers, Rodinò, Togliatti and Mancini, together with Morelli, now Cabinet Secretary, and for more than four hours the programme was read, re-read and mouthed, in order to introduce a few little phrases, suppress a few others, and modify a word here and there. But substantially my script remained intact. Extremely tired and bored by the thought that perhaps to-morrow, in Salerno, at the Cabinet meeting, there will be a repetition of criticism of this or that word, I worked a little in the evening on literary matters, for comfort.

April 27th

Left for Salerno accompanied by Innocenti, Badoglio's *chef de cabinet* whom I knew in Naples when he was secretary to the High Commissioner Castelli. He is a most capable functionary, and when the King had transferred himself to southern Italy and everything was lacking, men, premises, paper, he set up the first skeleton of the present Ministry (Badoglio once said to me that he had arrived in Brindisi with nothing but a pencil). Just now there is a strong current of opinion against Innocenti and people are asking that he should be removed from office, accusing him of Fascism. I don't know what weight can be attached to such accusations; but I think one should go slowly when they threaten to deprive the administration of able persons. The Cabinet met at 10 o'clock and after discussion, lasting two and a half hours, the programme was approved with only minor verbal alterations.[27] Went to lunch with Sforza and Omodeo and a journalist friend who had come from Naples. At 2 p.m. another meeting of the Cabinet. Badoglio gave a clear and detailed picture of the state of the Italian Armed Forces, and of Anglo-American and especially English opposition to our request for arms, and their unwillingness to use our troops, preferring to set them to work in the rear of the lines where the many unemployed would do equally well. This the Allies do, although they praise our airmen highly. They use the few planes left to them with great enthusiasm and to the utmost, so that very soon these will be worn out and useless. He also informed us of the new attitude to Russia. He read the Ministers an important letter from Roosevelt, binding us to alliance if a democratic Government is formed in Italy, and he has told Roosevelt that this has now been formed. A great scandal has arisen over the interview granted by the Prince of Piedmont to the London *Times,* in which, among other things, when asked how on earth Italy came to declare war on Great Britain and France, he replied that Mussolini wanted this and that the people consented, as was proved when no voice of protest was raised and no demand that Parliament be convoked! As though any protest could have been made, given the general enslavement of the press, and as though Italy still had a Parliament, when the Chamber was no longer called 'of Deputies' but 'of Fascios and Corporations' and consisted of men nominated by Mussolini himself, shuffled about or replaced according to his arbitrary will or caprice! All this the Prince could not or should not have ignored; ignorance in a case like this would be far worse and more negative than lies and sophistications to excuse the Monarchy. If this interview had come to my attention yesterday, before I received the Prince's visit, I would have spoken to him of it in strong terms.

April 28th–29th

Took a literary breath: among other things reread *El convidado de piedra,* attributed to Tirso de Molima, and got a clearer opinion of it.

[27] It can be found in vol. cit., pp. 72–4.

April 30th

Omodeo came and I exchanged ideas with him on various questions concerning the Ministry, and made certain arrangements with him. I think he has grown calmer and has reawakened the confidence which I have always had in his inner moral character and in his robust intelligence; I think he will make a good showing in matters of education and in the general affairs of that Ministry. I asked him to speak with Badoglio to-morrow, also in my name, about the news given in the papers by one of the Socialist Ministers of how the consultative assembly is to be formed; the matter has not even been discussed in the Cabinet and far less its composition: and to speak even more energetically of the Prince of Piedmont's interview with *The Times*, which can do great harm to Italy. Several visitors came, asking for recommendations, which I refused to make. In the evening sketched out a critical essay on the *Convidado de piegra.*

May 1st

The Prince's interview in the *Times* deeply troubles me. I have arranged, by means of the clandestine wireless which Raimondo uses for his Partisan work, to recommend the Milan Committee of Liberation to join with us in denying the Prince's words to the Allied Powers. But I refused to speak on the Naples radio to the Italians in German-occupied regions about the work of the Cabinet which we have formed. Sprigge came, together with an American journalist, Edgar Mowrer, whom I had known in Rome in 1932 and with whom I spoke of Italian matters and of what has happened here since July; he shares our ideas and preoccupations and believes that Volunteer Corps must be formed. He mistrusts Badoglio and on this point I was able to reassure him somewhat. Of Sprigge, who is very lukewarm or cautious, but an old and friendly acquaintance, I asked, jokingly, whether he could overrule his English Conservative tendencies and get published a reply of mine to the interview with the Prince of Piedmont. He immediately consented and we agreed to meet early on the day after to-morrow, when I will give it to him. When something has to be done which seems necessary I cannot urge others on, even from the highest motives, but I always end by remembering the proverb, "He who wants something goes for it, he who does not want something sends for it."

May 2nd

Wrote the essay on the *Convidado de piedra*. These delvings into the past are not just amusement, but refreshing waters which corroborate all the various activities in which I have to engage. They at once make me feel stronger, almost cheerful, more able to carry burdens and be annoyed. In the afternoon I took a walk.

May 3rd

Worked for more than an hour preparing the third and fourth number of the *Critica* for 1944. Wrote the protest against the Prince of Piedmont's interview, to give to Sprigge. I foresee that if it is published the Monarchists will react angrily, but come what may the country comes first in this most delicate moment. A visit from the Magistrate and President of the Court of Cassation, Casati, who was Minister of Justice in Badoglio's Cabinet and who brought me a copy of his Decrees on epuration, which have since been criticized and enlarged by other Decrees made by Neapolitan Jurists, who work on the principle of the non-retroactivity of law, a principle (Casati says) which they cannot believe a magistrate like him would ignore or despise. But this is a political as well as a juridical question, so much so that the new Decrees, in taking account of this, are for the most part contradictory. Casati explains the different attitude of the Southern lawyers by the fact that there were no spectacular Fascist crimes down there, and the mildness of the atmosphere tempered local Fascism, while in northern Italy, unless the accused are brought before regularly constituted tribunals, there will be massacres and crimes. These seem serious considerations to me and must be discussed in the Cabinet when the appropriate Decrees are drawn up. Maestro Angelo Lanza, who has been in America for six years, spoke to me about forming a Volunteer Corps (for which he wants approval of the Government) with Ettore Viola as Commander, a gold medallist[28] from the last war, fresh from America. I have promised to talk to Badoglio and my friends about it. He was accompanied by young Antonio Franchini, a Neapolitan painter and a comrade-in-arms of Alfonso Casati in the Grenadiers, still in Sardinia. Franchini has come to Naples on short leave to see his family. He told me about Fascism, indeed about a growing Fascism, among the officers of his regiment. This is not born, as Alfonso thinks, out of pure political passion but from

[28] The Italian equivalent of the V.C. Tr.

the inability to continue fighting, a fatal consequence of the dictated armistice and one which England and America wanted for their own ends. Alfonso is panting with desire to take an effective part in the war now in progress, and has asked for leave to come to see me about it. To-morrow I shall see whether Badoglio can get the leave through and send him to me. Looked through papers for the Cabinet and made notes on various points.

May 4th

Went to Salerno at 7.30 a.m. and came back at 8 p.m., accompanied by Eugenio della Valle. Two long sessions of the Cabinet. At the beginning of the first session Badoglio warned the Ministers against making any individual communication to the public or press about Cabinet meetings, and even more against making predictions about matters which have still to be discussed. The Socialist colleague, who felt himself reproved, excused himself for what had happened. Badoglio told us that he had spoken to the King about the interview given by the Prince of Piedmont, and that the King would forbid the Prince to give any more interviews or public expressions of opinion. I observed that this reassured us for the future, but could not cancel the past and that the interview published in *The Times* did great harm to the cause of Italy. I added that since the Prince had decided to enter the lists of journalism, I who can also be a journalist on occasions reserved to myself the right to reply on the same footing. This I declared out of courtesy to my colleagues, who received it in silence, without objections. In actual fact, a few moments before I had handed my reply to Sprigge in the Cabinet secretary's office, and he, having read it, had found it most lucid and succinct and had said it would be published.[29] Arangio Ruiz, Minister of Justice, criticized Casati's proposed law and supported the one drawn up by Ugo Forti and Enrico Altavilla, but other Ministers, and all of us finally, including Arangio Ruiz, preferred to start from Casati's premiss and consider epuration as a political procedure. It was decided that the Act of Epuration should be distinguished by three processes: (1) so-called 'defascistisation,' as it is now called, i.e. the dismissal from the Ministries and from local and parastatal administrations of employees who have been gravely compromised with Fascism, and of whom it may be said that they have retained its attitude and spirit; this action is already

[29] See in vol. cit., pp. 75–6.

under way with Omodeo as Commissioner; (2) so-called 'epuration' of other than State employees who are similarly compromised and deemed dangerous, against whom administrative measures must be taken, such as police supervision or confinement with certain limits; (3) punishment for the crimes of Fascism, to be extended to court cases which have ended in acquittals or amnesties, or which have simply been quashed and must now be re-opened. A committee of Ministers was formed to revise Casati's project in some of its details. It will come up for discussion and approval next Thursday. Generally speaking, up to the present the Cabinet procedure is good, the discussions are fruitful and lead to practical conclusions. Back in Sorrento in the evening I heard that Sprigge had been there at about 4 p.m., together with the correspondent of *The Times,* to assure me that the interview had seemed so serious to the latter that he had resubmitted it to the Prince, who had (himself or through his spokesman) reconfirmed it in every word and passed it as most accurate. Worked on the revision of proofs and on literary matters until after midnight.

May 5th

A bad day because of many callers and chatterers, from whom it is difficult to protect my work.

May 6th

A visit from Colonel Rodrigo, who is head of a delicate war service, and two of his companions. In the evening crowds of friends and acquaintances from various parts. Although we have lengthened the table, we do not know how to get any more chairs round it for meals. These are difficult problems of hospitality with which, at least until now, Adelina has always coped admirably.

May 7th

Visit of a Committee of the Publishers' Association in Naples to protest against the serious confusion caused by the Allies this year in school books. Wrote to Poletti about this. Went with my daughters to the unveiling ceremony of the memorial tablet in the house where Roberto Bracco died. Morelli brought me important documents, among them the text of the armistice, which Badoglio has not shown to the Ministers but wants me to see. Discussed the attitude we should take to the Prince of Piedmont. Views differed and clashed. But I agree with Sforza's idea, which he told me in the evening before going back to Naples, which is to get Badoglio to ask the Prince to change his whole military court and to take a civilian Minister or Secretary who meets with the approval of the democratic Cabinet. This was the advice which I gave the Prince in the course of our conversation, and even now it would strengthen us for the future and would appear as an implicit rejection of the past. That interview must have been the product of the surroundings in which the Prince lives, which do not sparkle with intelligence.

May 10th

Went on reading Goethe, all of whose works, especially the minor ones, I hope to reread.[30] Lanza and Ettore Viola came back about the formation of a Volunteer Corps. I must talk about it to Badoglio again, now that they say they have seen Macfarlane and got a half promise that the Allies will not raise any objection.

May 11th

Went to Salerno this morning. Talk with Badoglio, who fully approved the declaration I sent to *The Times* and says that I alone could usefully make it on account of my known monarchical sympathies. Now he wants me to help him in winding up this grave matter. As to the Volunteer Corps, I observed that even if nothing is done about it because of Allied opposition, it would be a good thing if he supported the proposal so as to bring out the Allies' real attitude towards Italy's desire to participate more fully in the war. Badoglio agreed and told me among other things that seven months ago the Allies limited the number of Italian combatants to only fourteen thousand, and that so far he has not been able to induce them to increase the number, not even now that a democratic Government has been formed. After long discussion in the Cabinet it was decided to publish a declaration regretting the form and the substance of the Prince of Piedmont's interview, and it was decided to press for radical changes in his court. I and the other Ministers without portfolio were charged with drafting a decree about the Consultative Assembly. The epuration decree was examined in detail and is now called " Epuration for crime and illicit gains under Fascism." I took part, insisting that any ruling of a retroactive

[30] From this re-reading came my *Terzi saggi sul Goethe*, part of the fourth edition of my *Goethe*, Vol. 2 (Bari, 1946).

nature should be taken out, as it was in Casati's first draft of the law. I also proposed, and it was approved, that no one could be denounced after a year. The death sentence, which the Fascist penal code restored, has been preserved because of the war, but only for Fascist crimes committed after the publication of that code. In due time and by a special decree the penalty will be abolished in the Italian code.

May 12th

At 11 a.m. the two Russian diplomats came and I talked with them for an hour and a half, telling them everything that I wanted them to know. They spoke in a generic and banal manner and I said I quite understood, that being diplomats they could not speak frankly, but that I, not being a diplomat, could say anything that came into my head.

May 13th

Got up early and noted all the parts of the speech I still have to write on the Italian political parties, and then make in Naples. But at 7.30 a.m. I had to interrupt my labours to go to Salerno. Two sessions as usual, but the second one shorter, so I could come back at 5 p.m. Main business: final revisions of the decrees about Fascist crimes, and grain prices. The Allies want to fix a price which all those who know anything about agriculture this year say is too low and will result in grave discontent and a black market. Four Ministers have been asked to see General Macfarlane about this, but there is little hope.

May 14th

Wrote the rest of my speech during the day: "The Liberal Party, its tasks and its relations with other Parties."

May 15th

Wrote to Morelli inviting him to come with friends, especially with De Nicola, to hear the speech on Saturday and criticize it. In the evening Raimondo gave me news of the patriots in northern Italy and proposed the formation here in Naples of a co-ordinating committee with the Allies and with Badoglio for the supply of arms and financial help to the fighters, also to watch over what is happening in Venezia Giulia, which Tito has occupied and where he is shooting any Italian patriots who show themselves. At first I welcomed this plan with enthusiasm, but I woke up in the night at four and re-examined the proposal and I discovered dangers, and the damage which might arise from the kind of people whom he wants on the committee, and I warned him about this and he could not gainsay my objection. Nevertheless he went to Naples to ask Sforza's opinion.

May 16th

A visit from a high official of the Ministry of Foreign Affairs and a long conversation, which brought light to bear on all the details of Italy's most difficult international position and on the painful position in which the Anglo-Americans have placed us, and our continual efforts to find a way out and to better them, which has so far met with little or no success. The lack of goodwill and the guarded answers, especially of the English, the popular hatred over there because of the many lives lost in the Mediterranean, are all increased by the lack of understanding and the slowness of their political representatives here, who administer affairs on the basis of a miserable armistice.

May 17th

The British Commissioner, Sir Noel Charles, who had made an appointment with me, came at about 5 p.m. and stayed for more than an hour in close talk. He met my observations intelligently, and with a friendly disposition. He recognized, as I do, the grave peril to which Italy is exposed and he hopes that the situation will soon get better and that Italy will achieve the status of an Ally. He assured me about the safety of Rome, which will be guaranteed against air attack, because the Anglo-American air defences are much stronger than the German attacks and because plans have been made not to occupy the city militarily.

May 20th

A visit from Berlinguer, Sforza's collaborator on epuration, and the new prefect of Bari, Lucifero, and Morelli, Ugo Forti and Calvi, and we had a long discussion about how the consultative assembly should be recruited. Received the terrible news that dear Leone Ginzburg, as a Russian subject, a Jew and an anti-Fascist, has been tortured in Rome prison and died there three months ago.

May 21st

Have been reading a most painful and serious book: *Con l'armata italiana in Russia*, clandestinely printed in Leghorn. Several Liberal friends came from Naples in the afternoon to look over my speech, and they all approved it. Asked Morelli to see Berlinger to-morrow and, on the basis of my remarks yesterday, to see whether any small revisions of the decree on Fascist crimes are necessary, so as to cancel any trace of retroactivity.

May 22nd

Studied papers outlining a Consultative Assembly and noted a few ideas on the subject. Visit from De Caro, former deputy for Benevento, with whom I discussed the fusion of the Liberal Democrats with the Liberals, since he is one of the principal representatives of the former in southern Italy. Sforza came and we talked of Italy's situation in the midst of these days' events, especially now that the new offensive for Rome has started. Tarchiani, the Minister of Public Works, has sent me a most urgent letter addressed to Badoglio in which he protests because the Allies keep our soldiers in places where there is no fighting and refuse to accept further troops who are now ready, in order not to overstep the small figure they have fixed. He proposes that we Ministers protest to the Allies and declare that, if things go on like this, we will resign. Sforza and I immediately supported this and a third Minister without portfolio, Mancini, having meanwhile arrived, also signed the letter. To-day we should have had a first go at the decree on the Consultative Assembly, but as Rodinò and Togliatti failed to appear, we exchanged ideas among ourselves without reaching any conclusions.

May 23rd

Left early for Salerno and before the Cabinet meeting saw Badoglio, who immediately told me that what we were asking for in yesterday's letter had already been granted as a result of his negotiations with the Allied authorities, and granted beyond our hopes: our contingent has been doubled from fourteen thousand to twenty-eight thousand combatants, and has been given important tasks at the front, so that even now it is fighting there with the other Allied forces. Moreover, three cruisers have been returned to us. I congratulated him and said that I hoped the service which he was giving to Italy would be recognized when we reached Rome, and with his usual simplicity, but with words which I shall not forget, more than courteous, affectionate, he replied: "Your appreciation is enough." Apart from these consoling declarations, we listened to a full report to the Cabinet by Orlando, the Minister for War, about the conspicuous work done these last seven months despite the difficulties which had to be overcome among the ruins and the deserts after the armistice. He also mentioned Italian officers who resisted the German invaders and read a long list of soldiers, Generals, Colonels and other ranks, whom the Germans shot or killed in various ways (in Albania hundreds were thrown into the sea with their hands tied!). As he named his comrades, Orlando was so moved that the tears came and he kept them down by drinking some water. I did not understand why Sforza thought it opportune, at the end of the report, after praising Orlando, to recommend the shooting of a certain number of Generals who surrendered their men and their arms without resistance, so as to make a necessary and expected example of them. I was not thinking of those who ought to be shot, but of those who are dead. I asked Rodinò, who was sitting near me, to reply and I expressed my feelings to Orlando after the Cabinet sitting. A declaration about our foreign policy, written by Sforza at the request of Badoglio, was read, and I asked him to take out some words about Italy promising to make reparations for misdeeds committed by our soldiers in places they have occupied, about which we have no certain proof. Also to take out a phrase about "abolishing the crime of war," because war is not a crime and cannot be abolished. Sforza agreed to both observations, because he is a good and loyal man, who sometimes lets himself be carried away by sheer impetus. At Omodeo's request several corrections were made in the 'defascistisation' decree (an ugly word which, although anti-Fascist, has a Fascistic sound).

May 24th

A young Italian in a Polish soldier's uniform came to see me. It was Second Lieutenant E.C., a Florentine, aged 24, who had been an interpreter at Lwow with the Italian Command in 1942–43 and had espoused the Polish cause. He was sent back to Italy and to Sardinia, and during a leave he had gone to a Polish Command and had himself sent to Tunis to join a Polish Corps. Now the Corps would not give him a commission, fearing diplomatic complications with Italy, and if the Army refuses to have him and send him to the

Front he is resolved to join the patriots in northern Italy, or to get himself taken away to Germany as a worker, then escape, and try to join the Polish patriots. To-morrow I will talk with Badoglio about it and hope he may find a favourable solution for the boy, who has a law degree and is well-read. I think some affair of the heart is involved in this adventure of his. In the afternoon the American Minister, Alexander Kirk, who had been in Italy for several years previously, came to see me and talked to me much about German and Italian things. Among other things he told me with much wisdom that the world will not find the right road unless it meets the pride and pomp of colossal and extraordinary actions with a 'humility,' that is at a Liberal pace, which is humble because it always seeks limited and modest tasks, discussing them scrupulously, applying them slowly, correcting and recorrecting them. He also told me that he had not yet found a convenient lodging, and that they want to requisition one for him, but that he feels a certain repugnance about it, because he has always been in the habit of paying rent for houses which he has occupied. I told him to watch over the fate of Rome, that it be not militarily occupied, and he is going to work for this, but he fears mines and, even more, German agents who may be hiding there. I urged him to get permission if he could for Del Secolo to travel about more freely and have more liberty in editing the *Risorgimento.*

May 25th

Cabinet meeting in Salerno: two sessions from 10 to 12 a.m. and from 2 to 5 p.m. Several decrees were approved. Lengthy discussion about the decree controlling agricultural rent. Here I noted (and Rodinò, Sforza, Arangio Ruiz and others supported me) for the sake of fairness something will have to be done about the landowners who collect their rents in money, for the rent value is going down, so that gradually they find they have nothing or practically nothing, while the tenants keep increasing their profits. The majority of the other landlords have arranged to take their rents in kind. This was met by the Communist Minister of Agriculture and by others with mere sophistry which I was easily able to confound, showing how this is not a question of favouring peasants but of favouring the tenants who are usually capitalists, so that the gratuitous wealth increase is of one capitalist against another capitalist. I modestly proposed that the question should be solved case by case, before

Provincial Committees consisting of a landowner, a tenant and a magistrate, who shall fix a just figure. They replied that the question was 'strictly political' (a parlance introduced by Fascism) and it was decided in the end to fix rents *ut sic* for another year; which is not a solution but an escape from a solution. I was sorry that Omodeo, although he recognized my reasons as good, came down on the other side because, he said, the provision in favour of a class of landowners would offend the employees who are asking and have not yet received higher salaries; as though the employees (who certainly have insufficient salaries, which must be increased as much as possible) were left stranded like those landowners at a figure fixed ten years ago, and as though one solution could impede or harm another. On this occasion I openly told my Communist colleagues that I do possess or rather administer lands which I gave my daughters twenty years ago, but that I am among the administrators with foresight who have chosen to take their rents in kind and not in money. This I did so that they should not drag me in as an 'agrarian' and so confute my logic, as they recently did when I defended Dialectics against the absurdities written about them by Lenin and Stalin.[31] I also proposed that the destruction of Fascist monuments, now going on in a chaotic manner and with danger of conflicts among the population, should be the subject of a decree and regulated by the Minister of Education, and through him by the Fine Arts depart-

[31] This was the only time I ever spoke on agrarian matters. But recently the fact was recorded inaccurately by Togliatti in an article which appeared as follows in all the Communist publications in Italy, great and small: "Alas! good Don Benedetto, half asleep at the Cabinet meetings, during that broiling May in Salerno, would wake up completely when agricultural contracts were discussed. Immediate interests of groups and of classes, in his case also, were vindicated by ideas which took precedence etc." (*Unità*, Rome, December 18th, 1946). And to think that I was always silent, even when the Minister of Agriculture proposed reducing rents in favour of the tenants and to the detriment of the landlords, with such illegal decrees that the Court of Cassation several times rejected them! But the amusing thing is that the point I made on May 25th in Salerno out of a simple sense of duty and justice, such as any member of a Government should feel towards all citizens indiscriminately, was adopted by the Communist Minister of Agriculture, Gullo, in his decree of April 5th, 1945, when I no longer belonged to the Government. By then he had made it his own, convinced by the evidence of the true state of affairs, but he went much farther than my first most modest proposal and ruled that rents should be paid which were equivalent to the value of rents paid in kind, and that moreover, public bodies of all kinds and charitable and benevolent institutions should have the right to get repayment on this basis for the previous year (see *Principal decrees of agrarian interest, emanated by Minister Fausto Gullo*, Rome, July 1945, pp. 12–15): a fact I discovered only later and by chance, when examining the balance sheet of an educational establishment in Naples, to whose governing board I belong. Really, I do not understand for what political reason Togliatti writes so much about me, so often, and such nonsense, when I do not allow myself such liberties about him.

ment, so as to preserve whatever is of artistic value or importance as well as curiosities in the way of historical documents. This was approved. After the second session of the Cabinet, we five Ministers without portfolio met to work out the composition of the Consultative Assembly, and when I had outlined the ideas discussed in our previous incomplete meeting, I was charged with preparing the draft of a decree.

May 27th

Outlined how the Liberal-Monarchical Party could fuse with ours. Meeting with Ugo Forti, Cassandro and Calvi to study the draft of the Consultative Assembly decree.[32] Prepared a small volume of my writings and political speeches during 1943 and 1944 for the publisher Ricciardi in Naples.

May 28th

Was shown a copy of the *Italia Libera* of New York, in which a journalist, Borgese, who was once Italian and is now an American citizen, throws insults at Sforza, Tarchiani and at me and says we are inferior in 'character' to the 'consistent Mussolini.' I am glad to have arranged matters happily with the Military for young C.

May 29th

Moravia, the novelist, came to Sorrento. He had to stay with his wife for several months on top of a mountain near Rome, but has now been liberated by the Allied advance. He poured out all his despair about the present and the future, nor was he able to produce anything more comforting than that.

May 30th

Revised the proof of a speech about the Parties and wrote, encouraged by friends and by Badoglio, another brief little speech for the opening of the Liberal Congress on the hatred which the world feels for Italy and on how we must behave in the face of it.

May 31st

Received a piece of comforting news to-day: Lieutenant Gallegos,

[32] The 'Consulta,' which we were planning in Salerno in May 1944, was not formed till a year later under Bonomi's Government.

the Englishman who came to fetch me to Capri last September together with Brindisi, and left Capri a few days later on a dangerous mission from which he did not return, so that he was believed killed, is alive and a prisoner of war in Germany.

June 1st

Cabinet meeting in Salerno from 10 a.m. to noon, and from 2 to 6.30 p.m. Friends to whom I showed my opening remarks to the Congress said they were well chosen.[33]

June 2nd

First session of the Liberal Congress in Naples. Back in Sorrento, I found two soldiers who had come on foot from Caserta, one of whom, a Leghorn man who said he was a relation of Modigliani's, and the other a Brindisi man, both anxious to fight and impatient about their enforced inactivity. They have had the bright idea of turning to me to get themselves sent into the line. I reproved them and explained that no one can interfere with the orders and dispositions of their superior officers and I persuaded them to return immediately to Caserta and make a clean breast of their escapade so as to lessen the punishment which they have deserved. As they asked me for it, I gave them a kind of statement about the motives which brought them here and about the advice I gave them.

June 3rd

Have written a 'Salute to Liberated Rome,'[34] which Del Secolo wants to have on hand for his paper, as he thinks the entry of the Allies into Rome is imminent. Duke Acquarone came from the King to ask me to arrange for him to be taken by air on the day when Rome is taken, so that he can put the date of Rome and not of Ravello (where he now is) upon the proclamation with which he will establish the Lieutenant-Generalcy. The message said that I was sure to understand certain delicacies of feeling which the politicians do not understand, and that, should the Allies object to this journey, he would be satisfied that the objection be stated when they communicate their reply to him, so that he should have a document showing that he was constrained to submit to their will. In conversation the Duke told me that the King did not abdicate, as he

[33] Gathered in the volume *Per la nuova vita dell'Italia*, pp. 77–80.
[34] In vol. cit., pp. 81–3.

should have done on July 25th last year when he dismissed Mussolini, because he deemed that his son, whom he had kept in the dark about affairs, was unprepared for, if not incapable of, the Succession. Concerning the scandalous interview of *The Times,* he further told me that the Prince had not in the least grasped the gravity of the declarations he had made and that several days were needed to make him understand. Acquarone concluded that the Prince will be docile, provided he is surrounded by the right people and provided he has a man of good will and intelligence to advise him.[35] The King also said that he would urge me to take over the Government of Italy, because he thinks that I alone have the necessary qualifications for this difficult task. If that were true! I promised no more than to do my best, after consulting Badoglio, to meet the King's wishes about the dateline on the proclamation. Other points which Acquarone touched upon were the strained relations between Badoglio and the King. I had begun reading again, and intended to get through my correspondence, thinking I would be left alone until to-morrow morning, when Dr. Morelli suddenly arrived and, with his usual affectionate concern, urged me to leave immediately lest I should not arrive in time to make my speech to-morrow. He said there were so many delays just now in car travel, owing to bad tyres, and the audience might wait in vain for my speech if I only left in the morning. Meanwhile Raimondo came with bad news about army matters and a forecast that there would be inevitable delays in the liberation of Rome, which might not take place for two or three weeks. Although Raimondo is never very fortunate in the news he collects, this time the King too is convinced, as Acquarone told me, that there will be at least a fortnight's time in which to prepare for his scheme to be carried out. All this saddened me, but since human judgment often errs and because of my old pedantic sense of order and precaution, I put the 'Salute to Rome' which Del Secolo asked me to write in my pocket and I left with Morelli. No sooner had I reached Naples and sat down to eat, than Del Secolo telephoned to say that the Allies will enter Rome to-night, and he asked me anxiously whether I had written the famous

[35] In publishing these details on their proper date, I feel, with due respect to truth, that I must add that my apprehension on account of that interview in the *Times* lasted several months, but that later, when I saw the Prince as Lieutenant-General several times for political consultations in 1945 and in 1946, I noted a gradual progress in his political formation. He listened carefully, asked serious questions, was constitutionally correct and showed a sense of personal responsibility lacking in him up till then because he had been kept away from the affairs of the people whose King he was called to be.

'Salute,' to which I was able triumphantly to bid him send round for it. I was the guest of Signora Sophia Bakunin for the night. She had often invited me to stay, and Sylvia came with me.

June 4th

Having reread and corrected the speech, I went to the Bellini Theatre at 10.30 a.m. It was quite full, perhaps more than 2,000 in the audience, and a scrum outside of those who would like to have got in. My speech was attentively followed and applauded at certain significant points.[36] At the end of it, Morelli arrived with the news of the Allies' entry into Rome, and with this news and the jubilations of those present, the Liberal Congress ended. I went to lunch with the American Ambassador Kirk, together with Morelli and Bergami. He had invited us. Then went to Altavilla's house, where the Sardinian Liberal delegates were waiting for me. Returned to Sorrento after 5 p.m.

June 5th

I woke with the intention of going to my desk and getting on with work which is behindhand, but at 7 a.m. a member of the Prime Minister's staff called for me in a car and took me to Salerno. As soon as I arrived I spoke with Badoglio of the King's wish and of other matters, among them the decrees which Poletti has put out for epuration in Naples, which differ from ours. The two hours' Cabinet meeting were devoted to arguments for and against the King's wishes, complicated by another request put forward by Omodeo and Tarchiani. They declared that their Party—always that brainless Action Party—wanted the Prince of Piedmont to withdraw from the Lieutenant-Generalcy (which is about to be bestowed upon him) in favour of the Duke of Genoa (whose reputation is not very striking). But how? Are we to send everything sky-high just at the moment when the King is carrying out what he undertook to do and what we accepted, when the Allies will not allow any alterations to what has been negotiated and agreed? This could only bring us an inevitable refusal and much mortification. And why was not this attempt—an attempt at the impossible—made when it would have appeared less unreasonable, when the Prince gave his interview to *The Times*? For my part I rejected the crazy demands of the Party of Action, which must have sent its orders

[36] The speech is in the vol. cit., pp. 119–36.

to its two Ministers, and left the question to the mercy of spasmodic agitations by others. I only suggested that humanity and 'kindness' —that 'Italian kindness' of which we are proud—should tend to make us agree to the King's modest request, which in the end merely amounted to this: that a refusal to comply with his desire, such as the Allies will almost certainly give, should reach him in writing. Although one of the Communists said, "Cortesia fia lui esser villano," I begged him laughingly to keep his Dante quotations for a better occasion, and when my motion was put to the vote it met with ten votes in favour and six against. There is no reason to suspect, as has been suggested, that the King has perfidious intentions of getting out of his undertaking. It is his natural reluctance to sign his proclamation in Ravello and his desire to sign it in Rome on his formal and almost symbolical return to the place where he was at the moment when the publication of the Armistice forced him to put himself in a safe place in southern Italy. Hardly had the session ended thus to my satisfaction, than Badoglio was called to the telephone. He came back to tell us that Macfarlane had made an appointment with him in Ravello for 3 p.m., with the King, who will evidently be made to sign the decree transferring his powers to the Lieutenant-General forthwith, bearing to-day's date and the name of Ravello as origin: so that not even this time will he receive Allied injunctions in writing. Not wanting to wait until evening for Badoglio's return, and feeling that there was nothing else of importance to settle, I went back to Sorrento.

June 6th

Read some noteworthy essays in manuscript by a young man in the Army who proves to be expert in history and philosophy and very intelligent. I shall try to get these published in some review. For the present, however, one cannot publish a true picture of the present conditions of the Italian Army, as he describes them in the longest of these essays. He tells of what he has seen and experienced these last eight months, and especially of what happened to officers and men under the German occupation, beginning with the Italians' behaviour and their fate in the Balkans, where he was on active service and a witness to it all. A committee of shipbuilders from Torre del Greco came to ask me to support a request for the return of the Italian Merchant Navy to the Ministry of Communications: a question I already know about and over which I have met the Admiralty's opposition. An American naval officer who does not know Italian or anything about Italy, but is a student of philosophy and political science, and anxious to get some clear ideas about Italy, brought me some important and recent American volumes. I gave him a book of mine, translated into English.

June 7th

Was told that the representatives of the six Parties in the Committee of Liberation in Naples are to leave for Rome by air. Meanwhile, Alfonso Casati suddenly arrived. I had been awaiting him after my exchanges with Badoglio and the Minister of War about his spending his leave from Sardinia with me, as he wished this. My joy was great and to-morrow I will be able to give personal news of him to Alexander and Donna Leopolda who have had no direct news of their son for ten months. Also I felt less anxious because I knew he wanted me to arrange for him to be sent to the front to fight the Germans and he counted on my co-operation for this, nor could I have withheld it or have opposed what he feels to be his duty, and yet I should then have shouldered a responsibility which properly belongs to his parents. Now he can open his heart to them himself.[37] Calvi, who is longing to see his wife whom he left in Rome five months ago, begs me to take him along and I have asked Badoglio to let him come, with the pretext that I need company and assistance. Badoglio said that even without a formal permit I could take him with me. Left in the evening for Naples, together with the Finance Minister, Quintieri, and slept in Sforza's house.

Rome, June 8th

With Sforza and Calvi went to Capodichino aerodrome and we left at 8 a.m., reaching Cisterna three-quarters of an hour later. From there by car to Rome and the Grand Hotel. Here, after a brief wait, I saw Bonomi arrive, also Casati, De Gasperi, Ruini and other Rome Party leaders, and Victor Emanuel Orlando, brisk

[37] Alfonso and his comrade-in-arms, Antonio Franchini, "one of those Neapolitans who are both joyous and melancholic and who know how to bind a friend with integrity of affection," came to spend a few days with us in Sorrento and then both left for the Front. A few weeks later Franchini fell, hit by a hand grenade, and "carried by Alfonso out of the lines, he spoke his last words of farewell and remembrance, and then Alfonso had to leave him and take his place again in the battle. When he got back to the spot later Franchini was already dead." Alfonso Casati himself fell on August 5th, he who "with his devotion to learning, his clear thinking, his proud character, his determination, and his proven devotion to his country, was one of those young men in whom we older men put our hopes for the revival of Italy. The loss of this young man is all Italy's loss." (Thus the obituary notice which is in my *Pagine politiche* (Bari, 1945), pp. 71–3.

despite his 84 years. Alessandro Casati's arrival was moving. He climbed the stairs of the hall in which I was, with tears in his eyes, and I waved a letter from his son and quickly told him that Alfonso was fit and well and with us in Sorrento.[38]

[38] At this point I end these diary extracts, having reached the end of that period during which Italy was represented only by us, who were then in the South. This Ministry governed despite all kinds of material difficulties (lack of offices, archives, experienced employees, Ministers' lodgings, and lack of good motor cars, for they travelled up and down from Naples for the most part), and managed to do a great deal of co-ordinated work, as appears even from these scanty notes. Their labours were achieved almost always by the cordial consent of all the parties, animated by a common enthusiasm for the new liberties. The diary goes on with a very detailed account of what happened when Bonomi's Government was formed, of its first crisis in November and December, 1944, its second crisis leading to the formation of Parri's Ministry (May–June, 1945), of the Parri crisis (November, 1945) opened by the Liberals, of the preparations for the Constituent Assembly and its election, and of the substitution of a Republic for the Monarchy (May–June, 1946), and so on, always sticking to facts with which the writer was personally concerned or which he himself witnessed. It seemed to me both useful and a duty to publish the exact details of what we did or tried to do during the Neapolitan period. For the rest, even if one need have no fear of contradiction, *per ignes,* when truth guides the pen, and although this later story would satisfy the curious (who, as such, are always somewhat petty) I do not think that any useful purpose would be served by publishing it. In the Naples days our minds were continually turned towards our like-minded comrades in Rome who were exposed to grave peril and had to hide, and we used to try to know their wishes by devious ways or we would guess their plans, and we always tried to let them see our work so that they could further it or suggest alterations. We knew by experience, through working and living in the open, many things which they, for nine months in the catacombs, ignored. They were shut up and much influenced by the place they were in, and a kind of half-presumptuous and half-factious spirit had grown up in some of them, so that we were received coldly and with diffidence and a kind of silent rebuke, as though we had travelled away from the straight road of which they alone possessed the key and knew the direction. I recall one small and significant detail of the welcome we got: when the list of new Ministers had been precipitately and somewhat roughly made, one of those who helped to make it dictated a communiqué for the Press, in our presence, with the heading "the first democratic Italian Ministry has been formed." At which the good Rodinò simply had to exclaim, "But this is an insult to us! What have we been doing, down in Naples? Do you think we made an aristocratic Ministry then?" The heading was withdrawn, but it reappeared all the same in the newspapers. When I tried to give some counsels of moderation they were not considered worthy of attention and the consequence of the lack of tact then shown towards the Lieutenant-General and towards Badoglio was immediate; General Macfarlane said that the new Ministry must go down to Salerno and start governing from there, after having taken over from the previous Ministry which reached Salerno on June 11th in the evening. But while the new Ministry was taking over on the 12th, an order came at noon to suspend everything, to leave the previous Ministry in office, and to await the *placet* of the Allies for the new Ministry. They had not taken the liberty of imposing any such *placet* upon us in April, so that we did not know that they could do so, and we went on with our sittings, but the new Ministry could not announce itself for several days. I then suggested, but in vain, that a solemn protest should be made to the Allied Government, despite the Armistice, for the Armistice had clauses which, despite their severity, never gave the right to violate the code of courtesy. A few weeks later, when the Ministry moved its seat to Rome, I handed in my resignation as a Minister without portfolio, preferring to participate in Italian political life to the best of my ability, but only as President of the Liberal Party and as a free writer.

APPENDIX

DOCUMENTS

I

REPORT AND PROPOSALS OF GENERAL DONOVAN, OFFICE OF STRATEGIC SERVICE

Salerno, September 23rd, 1943.

Subject.—Organization of Italian Operational Groups for Employment with Allied Forces.[1]

To Lt.-Gen. Mark W. Clark

(Through Maj.-Gen. Alfred M. Gruenther.)

From William J. Donovan, Director of Strategic Services.

1. Yesterday, together with Lt.-Col. John Whitaker, I talked at Capri with Benedetto Croce, well-known Italian philosopher and writer.

2. Mr. Croce, since 1924, has been the most courageous, aggressive and effective opponent of Fascism. By published articles and open statements he has denounced totalitarianism and attacked Fascist rule in Italy. The regime feared to arrest him. He has taken refuge in Capri only at the insistence of Allies, in order to avoid capture by the Germans.

3. In the course of our talk, Mr. Croce analysed the present psychological state of the Italian people, including their political thinking and their present attitude towards the war. We asked him what he considered the one most important means of fusing his people and restoring their self-respect.

4. His reply was instant and unequivocal. It is to give them the opportunity to enlist voluntarily in a fighting force under their own flag and fight by the side of the Allies.

5. I respectfully endorse these views and suggest that this would be a means of establishing a focal point for resolving the present difficulties and uncertainties of the various political elements of Italy; would bring to one place the residue of the fighting spirit; would serve to bind the people to the Allies; would give some

[1] See Diary entries from September 22nd to October 12th.

assurance of earning the right to free elections in the selection of their own government and would symbolize their consolidated active resistance to Germany and the German Army.

6. In principle, I recommend the following manner of organization:—

(a) to select a well-known Italian, with a military background, as the titular head, such as Maj.-Gen. Pavone, a pronounced anti-Fascist with an excellent record in the last world war and a man of reputation and standing.

(b) to provide for the assimilation of these volunteers as a fighting force under the rules of the Geneva convention.

(c) to give these volunteers the right to carry the flag of their own country: Italy.

(d) that instructors from SOE and OSS be attached to these groups for training in modern methods of demolition and in the tactics of irregular warfare.

(e) that for the purpose of obtaining immediate organization and employment of these groups, the Office of Strategic Services is prepared to make available such funds as may be necessary, and although I have not had opportunity of seeing our British colleagues, I believe they would also contribute.

Respectfully submitted,
WILLIAM J. DONOVAN.

II

CAPRI, IN THE HOUSE OF SENATOR CROCE

September 24th, 1943.

To (General Eisenhower) A.F.H.L.
From the National Front of Liberation.

1. Following the conversation at Capri between Gen. William J. Donovan, Director of Strategic Services, and Senator Benedetto Croce, following also the conversation at Paestum between Gen. Pavone, Avv. Mundo (Raimondo Craveri) and American and British representatives, the Executive Committee of the Fronte Nazionale della Liberazione has been established. The Executive Committee is composed of Sen. Benedetto Croce, Gen. Pavone, Alberto Tarchiani, Tenente Mundo. As soon as contacts are established the Executive Committee of the Fronte Nazionale della Liberazione will be enlarged in such a way as to include the repre-

sentatives of all the forces of Liberation now existing organized, and of those which may arise in various parts of Italy.[2]

2. (There followed Donovan's points, referred to in the previous documents. This document, signed by Croce, Pavone, Tarchiani, Craveri, was sent to Colonel Huntingdon and Major Munthe with an explanatory note, c/o 5th Army H. 42.)

III

Conversations with Marshal Badoglio in Brindisi
Letter from B. Croce to Badoglio

Capri, September 30th, 1943.

Illustrious Colleague,

Alberto Tarchiani and my son-in-law, Dr. Raimondo Craveri, bring you this letter and I would ask you to listen to what they have to say. Like every Italian who cares deeply for the dignity and future of his country, I can think of nothing else, these last two months, than of how Italy could play an armed part in the war which shall drive the Germans from our soil, and I feel in this matter that I interpret the intention of the policy which you have embarked upon. When talking a week ago with a high American authority who kindly came to see me, I could not refrain from expressing this Italian desire of mine. My hopes were not dashed and something was borne of it, as you will see from the accounts and the documents of the bearers of this letter. My idea and that of my friends was put down in an appeal written by me for publication, at the right time I hope, with the approval of the Allies. Will you read it and tell me what you think about it and then arrange with the bearers and give them instructions accordingly? They are fellow-members with me of the Committee of the National Front of Liberation. With our best wishes believe me,

Your devoted servant,
Benedetto Croce.

IV

Visit to Badoglio

Brindisi, October 4th, 1943.
3.17 p.m.

1. We were immediately ushered in to Marshal Badoglio, after

[2] This is the original text in English. Tr. I have not corrected it.

being announced by Colonel Valenzano. Badoglio got up and came towards us holding his hand out cordially and he used the 'voi' in talking to us.[3] We always used 'lei' when addressing him.

Dr. Craveri read Benedetto Croce's letter of introduction to the Marshal and then went into detail about the matters mentioned in the letter. He explained how General Donovan had been in Capri on September 22nd and had talked with Benedetto Croce, from whom the idea had originated of creating an Italian armed force alongside the Allies, and how he, Craveri, had seen Donovan again on September 24th at Paestum. For greater clarity he translated Donovan's letter to General Clark, Commander of the Fifth Army on September 23rd, advising the constitution of an Italian volunteer corps, under the Italian flag, commanded by General Pavone.

Commenting on the letter, the Marshal observed with great frankness that the Anglo-American Military Offices and their Generals often take contrasting and different courses with the result that tension and divergencies often arise among the various commanders. At that moment there were two Generals in Bari, one of them, Macfarlane, with the job of applying the decisions taken in the course of his conversation with Eisenhower in Malta. Macfarlane had assured him that all Italian military problems, as well as the rebuilding of the armed forces dependent on the legal Government of the King and Badoglio, would be dealt with by that mission (composed of two Generals and various officers), which alone had the authority to deal with these questions together with the Marshal and his Staff.

Tarchiani observed that Donovan was not only the General in command of Strategic Services but also a man of considerable political influence in the United States, personally friendly with Roosevelt. One might therefore suppose that he would be sufficiently authoritative to suggest and obtain a solution to the problem of Italian volunteers.

The Marshal then declared that he himself was trying to organize an advance corps of regular army soldiers, especially suitable for assault. For this purpose he was recruiting soldiers, sailors and airmen, especially from the north, men who had come south and who wanted to co-operate from a natural impulse in the Liberation of the north. He was setting up a body composed of four battalions,

[3] The second person plural, the 'voi' had been made compulsory under Fascism. The more courteous 'lei,' comparable perhaps to the Irish use of 'yourself,' has since come back into use.

six batteries, with armoured car, engineer and sabotage sections, etc. This body, which might be called 'a little division' rather than a regiment, would fight alongside the English. The chief difficulty lay in transport, because the English do not go on foot and one cannot keep up with them without lorries. He was collecting transport bit by bit, with great difficulty. At least four hundred vehicles were needed. The little division would be commanded by an Italian General and would fight under our flag.

In his conversation with Eisenhower, Badoglio had received permission to arm Italian combatant units, but with Italian arms and supplies which might have fallen into Allied hands in Sicily or in Africa. Badoglio described our armaments as antiquated and out-of-date. There were 1891 rifles and the artillery was in part captured material from 1918. With such arms the units he was building could not compete with the British in efficiency or speed, given the high-grade of motorization and mobility of the Allied troops. The King, who had been in Foggia, had told him that he had seen more than five thousand vehicles there.

2. Returning to the question of volunteer troops, Tarchiani said that we had gone to Brindisi to inform the Marshal of our plans. We did not want foreigners to get an idea of a two-fold action, or of any intention on our part to act unbeknown to the legal Government or in opposition to it. The immediate and sole aim was to fight for the Liberation of the country. The Marshal replied that he would always support any organization intended to throw the Germans out of Italy. We agreed that Germany was already 'smashed.' But the Germans were good soldiers and the battle was hard. If the volunteers fell into German hands they would certainly be shot. He added that the Germans were barbarians and he said it straight from the heart, but they were excellent fighters. Therefore he was doubtful not about the enthusiasm, but about the steadiness of volunteers under such conditions, over prolonged periods. One would have to be very prudent in order not to cut a poor figure. Craveri replied that loyal men, suitable for guerilla warfare, were to be had. The Marshal observed that the guerilla unit must be small and fast, for use especially on the Appenine range and in Abruzzo.

Tarchiani observed that we were concerned also lest the usual Communist elements take the initiative in forming action squads, because such bands would have a serious political effect later on. The Liberation Front's units would not contrast with the army formations organized by Marshal Badoglio, because anti-Fascist volunteers generally had political tendencies which made them unsuitable for membership of regular Governmental military formations, especially at the present time. What mattered was that Marshal Badoglio, if asked, should reply that any plan useful to the liberation of the country would meet with his approval.

Badoglio replied that if the heads of Eisenhower's mission asked his opinion, as they might, he would reply that he knew nothing about it, because it could only be officially communicated to him by the Allies. Tarchiani insisted on the non-political nature of the plan and its immediate anti-German military objective. He asked the Marshal not to stick at a negative opinion, but to recommend and favour our plan as much as he could, for it was intended as co-operation in the task of Italian liberation which ought not to be a monopoly of foreign armies. The Marshal then explicitly declared that he would gladly express a favourable opinion about our plans.

3. During the conversation other questions were discussed, especially Fascism, and the war, political parties and internal policy, the Monarchy and the Government's foreign policy.

4. *Foreign Policy.* Badoglio said he took the reigns of Government on July 25th in obedience to the King, because he had never yet refused a task given him by the King.

But the immediate and serious problem was to end the war. Steps in his foreign policy had been as follows: the war, the armistice, collaboration, co-belligerence, alliance with the Anglo-Americans. He was glad to have reached the stage of co-belligerency, and he wished and hoped soon to achieve alliance. He had said to Eisenhower that he wanted to fight both Germans and Fascists, for the latter had become traitors to their country. At this point he referred to the position of Graziani and of Mussolini. He told of the 'tragic flight' from Rome. A convoy of cars had left the capital in the early hours of the morning. Behind the Marshal's car came the car of the King, the Queen and Prince Humbert. They met German armoured cars coming towards the city, and they crossed the German line and finally reached Pescara. There they embarked on a corvette waiting for them. At sea, a German aeroplane flew over and must have seen that there were many people on the vessel. An air attack was expected but fortunately did not take place. Off Bari, a submarine warned the fugitives that the city was in German hands. The corvette sailed on to Brindisi and learned that 'there was no one there.' So they landed.

5. *Fascism and the War.* The Marshal said that everything was corrupt in Italy. He had ordered an administrative inquiry which revealed that the G.I.L. ('Lictor's Youth Groups') cost nearly 1,700 million a year, the OND (Workers' Recreation Club), 1,200 million. The AGIP (Italian Petroleum Trust) had a deficit of 90 million yearly. He talked of the discussions in the supreme Military Council, where he had maintained that the war would be long and difficult, because England tends to turn these conflicts into long drawn-out efforts, which bring exhaustion to the enemy. To illustrate the incompetence of Ministers who should have prepared the country for war, he described an argument with 'that thief' Riccardi. Badoglio had taxed the Exchange Minister with incompetence and lack of authority in war preparations. He asked him whether he could furnish 42 million pairs of boots to the Army (as many as had been needed in the first world war), and at the same time satisfy the needs of the civilian population. This was a detail, but it served to show the incompetence of the Minister, who had never thought of the problem.

He spoke of his resignation during the war against Greece, and referred to his reply to the 'stationmaster of Cremona' (Farinacci),[4] who had accused him of having misused army funds. He said that as Chief of the General Staff he had nothing to do with balance sheets and with the use of monies by the Military Departments.

When Tarchiani suggested that big sums for defence had been turned to Fascist uses, Badoglio replied that he had never had any jurisdiction over military budgets.

He further said that the war had been declared irresponsibly by Mussolini alone, without the consent and against the will of the peoples. No war could be won under such conditions. The only obstacle to peace was therefore Mussolini, and so he was removed. Political and military forces had been ripe for the *coup d'etat.* The latter played the decisive part.

6. *Parties and Internal Policy.* The Marshal counted the five Parties on the fingers of his hand. Then he said that only the Christian Democrat and the Communist Parties have General Staffs and troops. The others only have General Staffs. They had not known how to organize the troops; 'nor have we Liberals.'

To show us how bothered he was by the Parties, he told us of an inter-Party delegation which had come to Brindisi offering its col-

[4] Farinacci, one of Mussolini's most violent supporters, had been the stationmaster of Cremona before the 1914 war. Tr.

laboration under certain unspecified conditions. With annoyance in his voice, the Marshal said that he had no use for that kind of collaboration and that he did not want to engage in negotiations with the inter-party delegation out of weakness, and that if he wanted to he could deal with the situation under existing martial law. He said he was seventy-two and that he presided over the Government temporarily and solely as a duty. In Rome the foundations of the Ministry would be extended to include all the representatives of the different political currents. He recognized that there was no Ministry in Brindisi but only a few military leaders. Referring to 'subversive' currents, he thought that the Allied occupation would last some years and would not create a situation favouring the development of certain ideas. He said he would resign as soon as the national territory had been freed from the Germans. "My profession is not that of a head of a Government." "It is not for me to make the elections." The Marshal was indignant about the rush for offices and especially for Trade Union and administrative jobs. He told how he had got 'angry,' unusual for him, and had roughly dealt with Party representatives who were trying to make him appoint certain persons to Trade Union jobs. He had told them that it was a sign of moral poverty, given the tragic situation of the country, to try to reap personal or Party or clannish spoils.

7. *The Monarchy.* Whenever the King was mentioned in the conversation the Marshal displayed an unalterable attachment to "His Majesty the King." He acknowledged quite happily that he had sent a circular to the prefects urging that only men "of ascertained Monarchist faith" should be chosen for Trade Union and administrative posts. Tarchiani drew the Marshal's attention to the fact that "Monarchist loyalty" could not be a guarantee of competence or of patriotism. For example, the Communists to-day say they are agnostics about the institutional question, to-morrow they may easily call themselves Monarchists. Their aim is to handle the levers of the machine and to maintain a weak Monarchy so as to be able the more easily to upset it. The Marshal replied that this danger had escaped his notice but that with strict control one might have two or three black sheep to ninety-seven white. Tarchiani replied that among those who question the Monarchy there are many excellent patriots. They must be used in the Liberation's struggle. It would be difficult for Badoglio to use them. But these three Italians could be gathered into the National Liberation Front.

8. *Sforza.* Tarchiani then spoke of the forthcoming arrival of

Count Sforza to see what the Marshal's reactions would be. Tarchiani exalted Sforza's love and devotion to Italy and the great services he might render the country. The Marshal said he knew Sforza well and had worked with him at Santa Margherita during the Rapallo Treaty negotiation, and esteemed him highly. "But he seems to have said in the United States that he did not want to take part in the Government." He added: "The King is against Sforza because of some critical articles printed in Brussels a few years ago. But I said to his Majesty that such questions were irrelevant in times like these, when one must swallow a lot.[5] The Marshal said that Sforza had great influence in the United States. This factor would have to be taken into account.

9. The Marshal read Croce's proclamation and fully approved it. But he observed that it would not be opportune to publish the passages which concerned his Government at once, because he could not even be aware of our intention until the Allies had definitely approved it. We gave him assurances about this.

Finally, Tarchiani summed up the nature and the value of the National Liberation Front's plan and repeated that the Government could not but be agreeable to an undertaking whose immediate object was the liberation of the territory, an object which was identical with that of Badoglio. Thus the Marshal was induced for the third time to say that he would be happy to pass a favourable judgment on it to the Allies.

As we took our leave the Marshal expressed most friendly feelings for Senator Croce.

ALBERTO TARCHIANI
RAIMONDO CRAVERI

V

MANIFESTO FOR THE CALL-UP OF VOLUNTEERS

Pasted up in Naples on October 10th, 1943

ITALIANS!

With the news of the Armistice made by us, the Germans occupied the greater part of Italy, proclaiming that every Italian, his life and his property, would be at the mercy of any German officer or soldier, and as proof and guarantee of the threat, they

[5] Badoglio used the Italian idiom *transgugiare dei rospi,* literally 'swallow toads,' but the implication was not that Count Sforza was a toad. Tr.

quickly gave us examples here of what they have already done in Poland, in Czechoslovakia, in France, in Russia and in Denmark. Wherever they have gone they have added new and frightful terrors to the old story of the barbaric invasion, which is the fount, still fresh and powerful, of their national boastfulness. Already the effect of their intentions is clear in places like Naples, which they held and then had to abandon at the point of Anglo-American arms. Here they blew up or burnt down public buildings, destroyed all the industries, even the non-military ones, emptied the store-houses of supplies, looted the shops and shot a great number of the citizens, taking others from the streets away to slavery.

Destruction, horror, pain are falling upon us: this is not a new situation. It existed from the very day on which Fascism made the so-called 'pact of steel' with Germany, against our whole national position, all our political and economic interests, our very geographical position, and not only against our past and our present, but against our future, because a German victory could only promise us subjection to the 'chosen' race, the lords of all Europe, who singularly despise and offend the *Welschen*, or us Italians. This was a stupid pact, a Party pact, openly made in the interests of a faction which had lost the support of all intelligent people, was void of all love or duty towards the country, and tried to insure itself with German strength. Then Italy was truly handed over to Germany under the designation of 'ally.' The Germans were introduced into every branch of our production and administration and occupied important cities and essential military positions. Their occupation was masked but effective. The armistice we have now made has merely torn the mask away and revealed the hypocrisy of this alliance.

Our people immediately realized the situation and our supposed allies, however great the reputation of their discipline and military ability, were in no single district of Italy received with the kind of sympathy and applause due to allies, like that which met the Italians in France when they went to fight at Bligny. German soldiers moved about our cold and diffident cities, feeling they were among enemies who would sooner or later turn against German aeroplanes, guns and machine-guns. On the other hand there was hardly an Italian family which did not listen anxiously, many times a day, to the forbidden wireless stations, following the progress of British, Russian and American armies with hope and deep feeling. This is the truth which every one can substantiate from private experience. In the soul of every Italian here in Italy two wars were already being fought: the war conducted by the Fascists and another war tenaciously in line with the spirit of the *Risorgimento*: the first was legal in appearance but odious, the second was dear to the heart of every true Italian.

Now that the mask is gone and the hypocrisy is revealed by predictable and inevitable events destruction and grief fall upon us, but the situation might be worse, and has in fact revealed our superiority, for now we no longer have to be patient, but we can work, answer back and fight. Already in every part of Italy our people are fighting back in the most varied ways. In Naples, men, women and children, with the few arms they could procure, displayed that heart and fighting spirit and spontaneous heroism which has always arisen in famous struggles against the foreigner in our city. The second war which we had in our hearts has now become legal, making the other war, declared by Fascism, illegal and criminal, despite all vain arguments since the Armistice to entice people to obey the German destroyers and butchers of the Italian people. Our war against the Germans is legal, for it is the policy of the only Government which now legally exists in Italy, the Government which made the Armistice with the Allies. We must gather all our forces for this war, for the honour of Italy, for the future of Italy. We must accept all the necessary pain, renunciation and sacrifice. This is in truth Italy's hour, not the hour in which Fascism prepared its brigand's attack on defeated France.

The hatred against the foreigner who kicks and insults Italy and against his accomplices, traitors of their country, is enormous among the young and the old around us. But equally great is the love for this unfortunate and noble country which did not deserve to be dragged where it has been dragged by its unworthy sons. Great is the enthusiasm and the loyalty which we see in people's faces, and there is a resolution and a certainty that our efforts will save and remake our fine country, not only for the glory of her arts, but for the clarity of her intelligence, her human kindness and understanding, and her respect for all peoples, according to the teaching and doctrine of the Italian, Giuseppe Mazzini.

The National Liberation Front composed of free citizens, united in a single sentiment of absolute and single minded devotion to their country, whose directing Committee speaks to you in this appeal, announces that Italian Combatant Groups under the Italian tricolour have been instituted to-day to co-operate with the Anglo-American armies to chase the common enemy from Italian soil. Their military Commander will invite you to enlist and give you the necessary details.

THE NATIONAL LIBERATION FRONT.

Naples.
October 10th, 1943.

BIOGRAPHICAL NOTES

ALBERTINI, ALBERTA. Joint editor of the *Corriere Della Sera* before Fascism, and brother of the proprietor of the famous Liberal newspaper (also a relative of the Croce family).

ALTAVILLA, ENRICO. A Liberal Neapolitan lawyer, and local leader of the Party.

AMENDOLA, GIOVANNI. A Liberal Deputy who was beaten up by the Fascists in 1925 and severely injured. Died later in exile as a result of his injuries.

ARANGIO, RUIZ. Professor of Roman Law. Several times Minister in post-1943 Cabinets.

BAKUNIN, SOFIA. Daughter of the anarchist Bakunin and wife of a Neapolitan lawyer called Caccioppoli.

BERGAMI, DR. Biologist. Local Neapolitan Liberal leader.

BLANCH, LUIGI. Neapolitan philosopher of the 18th century.

BOGOMOLOV, ALEXANDER. Soviet representative at Allied Forces Headquarters, first in North Africa and then at Caserta.

BONOMI, IVANOE. Prime Minister of Italy 1921–22, sometime Reformist-Socialist. President of the Committee of Liberation in Rome 1943–44.

BRACCO, ROBERTO. Playwright who met with success in the early years of the century but abandoned the theatre because of Fascism.

BRINDISI, AVVOCATO. Neapolitan lawyer, friend of the Croce family and Mayor of Capri after the fall of Fascism.

CALVI, ANTONIO. Journalist. Member of the Rome Liberal Party, which sent him south, across the lines, to visit Croce.

CAMERINI, DUKE. Venetian gentleman, sent to 'confino' for anti-Fascism and liberated by the Allies.

CARACCIOLO, FILIPO. Neapolitan Prince, diplomat. Held post as Under Secretary in Badoglio's first Government. Was the Naples leader of the Action Party.

CASATI, ALESSANDRO. Anti-Fascist senator. Minister for war after the liberation.

CASSANDRO, GIOVANNI. Neapolitan lawyer. Representative of the Liberal Party.

CIANCA, ALBERTO. Editor of the Radical newspaper *Il Mondo* until its suppression by Mussolini in 1926. Then went into exile first in Paris and then in the U.S.A.

CIFARELLI, MICHELE. Young Bari magistrate and leader of the Action Party in Bari and later of the Republican Party.

CRAVERI, RAIMONDO. Son-in-law of Croce. Head of the Research Department of the Banca Commerciale Italiana. At the end of the war, partisan General, liaison officer with Allies.

CRAVERI, CROCE, ELENA. Eldest daughter of Croce. Born 1915, wife of Raimondo Craveri and mother of Piero and Benedetta. Took law degree at Naples University, specialised in German literature, founded a magazine, *Arethusa,* and later the *Italian Spectator.*

CROCE, ADELE. Wife of the philosopher, born Turin, took degree at Turin University and was an active Social worker until Fascism forbade her association with an Institute which she ran in Naples. Mother of Croce's four daughters.

CROCE, ALDA. Second daughter of the philosopher, born 1918, took degree in literature at Naples University. Specialised in Spanish literature and has published two books on the baroque poet, Gongora, and on Lopez de Vega. Now wife of Franco Carandini.

CROCE, LIDIA. Third daughter of the philosopher, born 1922. Took degree in philosophy at Naples University. Has written literary articles, and translated books from the German. Married to a young historian, Vittorio de Capraris.

CROCE, SILVIA. Fourth daughter of the philosopher, born 1923. Took her degree in history at Naples University.

DE CESPEDES, ALBA. Popular Italian writer and journalist of Cuban origin. Editor of *Mercurio,* a new literary monthly, in 1944.

DE GASPERI, ALCIDE. Born 1882, in Trento. Represented his native province when it was still under Austria in the Imperial Parliament in Vienna. Member of the Popular Party during the rise of Fascism. Spent the years of the Dictatorship working in the Vatican Library. Leader of the Christian Democratic Party and Prime Minister of Italy 1946–

DE NICOLA, ENRICO. Famous Neapolitan criminal jurist. President of the Italian Chamber in 1922. Has the reputation of never having defended a man in court whom he knew to be guilty. Elected by both houses to be Provisional Head of the Italian Republic immediately after the plebiscite of June 1946.

DE RUGGIERO, GUIDO. Author of the classical *History of Liberalism* and professor at Rome University before and after Fascism. Died 1948.

DEL SECOLO, FLORIANO. Neapolitan journalist. Senator of the Popular Front in 1946. Died 1948.

EINAUDI, LUIGI. Distinguished political economist. Piedmontese. Liberal. President of the Italian Republic 1948–

FLORA, FRANCESCO. Anti-Fascist philosopher and historian of literature. Now professor of Italian literature at Milan University.

FORTI, UGO. Professor of Administrative Law, Naples University.

GINSBERG, LEONE. Russian Jew, naturalised Italian, poet and anti-Fascist. Died in prison after torture 1944.

GREENLEES, IAN. British major in charge of broadcasting to Italy 1943–44.

GULLO, FAUSTO. Calabrian landowner. Communist. Minister of Agriculture in the first Bonomi Cabinet.

IMBRIANI, VITTORIO. Neapolitan writer on the Risorgimento.

KIRK, ALEXANDER. American envoy, later Ambassador, to the Kingdom of Italy 1943–46.

KOSTYLEV, MIHAIL. Soviet Ambassador to the Kingdom of Italy 1943–46, reconfirmed Ambassador to the Republic 1946–

LANDI (SISTER) MARIA. A sainted nun alleged to have the stigmata.

LATERZA, GIOVANNI. Head of Croce's publishing house, and publisher of most non-Fascist literature during the Dictatorship.

LUCCETTI. Italian anarchist once author of an attempt on Mussolini's life.

LUCIFERO, SENATOR. Monarchist journalist and politician.

MACMILLAN, HAROLD. British Minister in the Near East 1942–46 and attached to A.F.H.Q. Member of Parliament (Conservative). Member of the famous publishing firm.

MANN, KLAUS. German author, son of Thomas Mann.

MASSIGLI, RENÉ. French envoy to the Kingdom of Italy, later Ambassador in London.

MATHEWS, H. U.S. journalist, represented the *New York Times* in Italy at various times and during the liberation, later in London.

MINIFIE, JOHN. Canadian journalist attached to the political warfare department of A.F.H.Q.

MORAVIA, ALBERTO. Italian novelist, several of whose works have been translated into English (*Augustino, the Woman of Rome*).

MORELLI, RENATO. Neapolitan Liberal leader, for some time Under-Secretary in Badoglio's Cabinet.

MORRA, UMBERTO. Tuscan Count, man of letters, private secretary to Badoglio's Minister Piccardi.

MOWRER, EDGAR. American newspaperman and author of *Germany Puts the Clock Back* and other political works.

MUNTHE, MICHAEL. Elder of Dr. Axel Munthe's two sons, both of whom were educated in England. Major in special force serving with the 8th Army. Dr. Axel Munthe was physician to the Queen of Sweden, who lived most of her life in Italy under his care.

MURPHY, ROBERT D. U.S.A. representative at Allied Forces Headquarters first in North Africa and then at Caserta.

NICOLINI, FAUSTO. Neapolitan scholar and specialist on Giambattista Vico.

OMODEO, ADOLFO. Anti-Fascist Sicilian historian, wrote notable works on the Resorgimento, the French Restoration and De Maistre. 1944 Rector of Naples University and 1945 Minister of Education. Died 1946.

ORLANDO, VICTOR EMMANUEL. Prime Minister of Italy 1918 and representative of Italy at Versailles Peace Conference. Last surviving member of the "Big Four" of that period. Sicilian, native of Palermo and Senator for that region in the Rome Senate, 1948–

PACKARD, REYNOLDS. Chief war correspondent for the United Press Agency in Italy before and after Fascism.

PARENTE, ALFREDO. Student of philosophy and music, Liberal Neapolitan leader, author of a work on musical æsthetics.

PARRI, FERRUCCIO. Anti-Fascist Republican leader. Head of the Research Department of the Edison Company in Milan during the Dictatorship. President of the Northern Italian Committee of Liberation and Deputy Commander of the Partisan Army under the German Occupation. Head of the Party of Action during its lifetime. Prime Minister of Italy for six months 1945–46.

POLETTI. U.S. Colonel, regional commissioner for Allied Commission first in Palermo, then in Naples and in Milan. Formerly Vice-Governor of New York State.

Reale, Eugenio. Communist representative on the Naples Committee of Liberation. Later, Italian Ambassador to Warsaw.

Rodino, Giulio. Neapolitan gentleman. Member of the Popular Party before Fascism and held Ministerial post. Returned to politics after the liberation serving as a Christian Democrat Minister without portfolio. Died 1947.

Rosselli, Carlo and Nello. Carlo escaped from island confinement by the Fascists in 1928 and founded the "Justice and Liberty" anti-Fascist movement of Liberal-Socialists in Paris. He was assassinated together with his brother by the Cagoulards at Bagnolles de l'Orme in 1936.

Ruini, Marcello. Son of pre-Fascist Minister Meuccio Ruini.

Salvadori, Max. Member of an Anglo-Italian family, served under the name of Captain Sylvester in the British Army behind the German lines. Brother of Joyce Lussu who made the journey from Rome across the German lines to visit Croce in 1943. Her husband sat for the Sardinian Party of Action before Fascism and now for the Sardinian Socialists.

Sforza, Carlo Count. Native of Liguria. Diplomat. Resigned post of Italian Ambassador in Paris on receiving news of march on Rome in 1922. Later went into exile in Belgium and the U.S.A. Author of several works on Italian history. Foreign Minister 1919 and again 1948–

Sheean, Vincent. American journalist and author, commissioned in the U.S.A.F.

Sprigge, Cecil. British journalist and author. Chief correspondent for Reuters Agency in Italy during the liberation. Husband of Sylvia Sprigge of the *Manchester Guardian*.

Tarchiani, Alberto. Anti-Fascist journalist who went into exile when the "Mondo" was suppressed by Mussolini in 1922. Later 1948– Italian Ambassador to the U.S.A.

Togliatti, Palmiero. Head of the Italian Communist Party since 1943, when he returned to Italy after many years' exile in Moscow where he became secretary of the Comintern. Togliatti is a native of Piedmont and a founder with Gramschi of the Italian Communist Party in Turin after the first World War. Under Fascism, Gramschi was tried and condemned to 30 years' imprisonment and died before the sentence was completed.

Vinciguerra, Mario. Italian journalist and author who was sentenced to 12 years' imprisonment by the Fascists for being associated with Lauro de Bosis' "National Alliance," in 1930. Later President of the Society of Authors.

WHITAKER, TOM. U.S. journalist.

ZANIBONI, TITO. Ex-Socialist deputy who served a long prison sentence on a charge of attempting to assassinate Mussolini. Became High Commissioner for "Epuration" in Badoglio's Government.

ZANOTTI-BIANCO, UMBERTO. Noted Piedmontese philanthropist and scholar who established dispensaries and schools in remote southern Italian villages under the auspices of Dr. Franchetti's "Southern Association." Archæologist and excavator at Paestum and Selinunte. Later President of the Italian Red Cross.